3 PARA
MOUNT LONGDON
The Bloodiest Battle

3 PARA
MOUNT LONGDON
The Bloodiest Battle

Written and edited by
JON COOKSEY

with contributions from:

John-Hughes Wilson • Tim Lynch • Terry Peck

Nick Rose • Michael Savage

Pen & Sword
MILITARY

First published in Great Britain in 2004
and reprinted in this format in 2017 by
Pen & Sword MILITARY
An imprint of
Pen & Sword Books Ltd
47 Church Street, Barnsley
South Yorkshire
S70 2AS

ISBN 978 1 47389 896 7

A CIP catalogue record for this book is
available from the British Library

Printed and bound in Malta by Gutenberg Press Ltd.

Pen & Sword Books Ltd incorporates the Imprints of Pen & Sword Aviation,
Pen & Sword Family History, Pen & Sword Maritime, Pen & Sword Military,
Pen & Sword Discovery, Pen & Sword Politics, Pen & Sword Atlas,
Pen & Sword Archaeology, Wharncliffe Local History, Leo Cooper,
Wharncliffe True Crime, Wharncliffe Transport, Pen & Sword Select,
Pen & Sword Military Classics, The Praetorian Press, Claymore Press,
Remember When, Seaforth Publishing and Frontline Publishing

For a complete list of Pen & Sword titles please contact
PEN & SWORD BOOKS LIMITED
47 Church Street, Barnsley, South Yorkshire, S70 2AS, England
E-mail: enquiries@pen-and-sword.co.uk
Website: www.pen-and-sword.co.uk

CONTENTS

ACKNOWLEDGEMENTS

I owe a great debt of thanks to the contributors who all threw their wholehearted support behind the project in 2004. The written and oral accounts of John Hughes-Wilson, Tim Lynch, the late Terry Peck, Nick Rose and Michael Savage helped to provide a much greater depth to the final product than I initially envisaged. All of them served during or immediately after the Falklands War and all were unfailingly helpful and punctual in producing their accounts and accompanying illustrations. I know it was difficult at times for some of them to speak with me and I appreciate their patience during my questioning.

My thanks also to Major General Julian Thompson, Commander of 3 Commando Brigade during the war, who, despite a busy schedule, found time to respond promptly and with candour to several requests for information and opinion. I am grateful that he also found time to read and respond to a draft on the section on 'The Preparations' for the battle.

Jon Wilkinson's eye for design and his skill in presenting the illustrative material in order to enhance and support the text, never fails to amaze me. I thank him for his talent and his patience.

Finally, my thanks go to my family; my wife Heather and my daughter, Georgia, who, as always, supported me during those times when, 'daddy went off to write about soldiers.'

Jon Cooksey
2017

INTRODUCTION

Think Falklands, think Parachute Regiment, think Goose Green. The connection is understandable. It is thirty-five years since the 2nd Battalion of the Parachute Regiment fought the Argentine defenders of the Falkland Islands settlements of Darwin and Goose Green and achieved a morale boosting victory at a heavy price - 15 dead, including their Commanding Officer Lieutenant Colonel 'H' Jones, and 32 wounded. Lieutenant Colonel Jones was later awarded a posthumous Victoria Cross for his actions during the battle.

It has been said that the battlefield of Darwin-Goose Green is now the most famous British battlefield of the second half of the twentieth century - most of the more than 40,000 tourists who journey to the islands each year visit it - and that the battle itself, the first set-piece battle of the Falklands war, is 'the most studied and analyzed battalion sized action in military history.' [1] This fact is undeniable as is its significance. Politically and strategically it brought the scramble for a peaceful comprise to a halt with a bloody jolt and cast the first shadow of defeat over the Argentine effort both in Buenos Aires and at their HQ in Port Stanley. For the rest of the British forces on the ground the victory at Goose Green set a morale boosting precedent for the four battalion sized battles to come. But the later battles each had their own particular 'texture' and intensity. Is Goose Green the most famous and the most studied simply because it was the first and because a commanding officer was killed in a charge against enemy positions, an action for which he later received a VC?

On the day that 2 Para was making its final preparations for the attack on Goose Green its sister battalion, 3 Para had moved out from its positions on the beachhead at Port San Carlos in a Tactical Advance to Battle or 'TAB' across East Falkland. On a miserable and spirit sapping journey, the news of 2 Para's victory a day later filled the men of 3 Para with pride. Twenty year-old Private Nick Rose of 6 Platoon in Major Mike Argue's B Company, recalled his feelings on hearing the news:

'They'd been committed and 'bang' they'd done it and it was "well done the blokes, well done Para Reg." We were so proud, but then sad because of the guys killed - and then scared! But hey, look, they've done it, we can do it and we're going to do it very soon so focus. Clean your weapon, keep your weapon dry if you can, sort yourself out and try and get your 'admin' done as much as possible. 99.9% of paratroopers hate 'admin', they're combat soldiers - they want to get on, do the job and let somebody else tidy up afterwards. We'll go on and do the next thing you want us to do but don't make us do all the shit afterwards.'

Rose and his comrades were highly trained, professional soldiers, determined to emulate the deeds of their sister battalion when their time came to prove themselves on the battlefield. And, just as they sensed, their time would come, two weeks later. Their battlefield would be in and among the long, frost shattered spines of rock which stabbed the air from the summit of Mount Longdon, one of the peaks that studded the outer ring of the Port Stanley defences. The battle for Mount Longdon deserves a place alongside Goose Green in the history of this illustrious regiment for it was a battle which tested the discipline, comradeship and professionalism of the paras to the limit; it was a battle which witnessed another posthumous para VC; it turned out to be the bloodiest battle of the entire Falklands campaign.

THE POLITICAL PROBLEM

I n August 1914 Britain went to war over a 'scrap of paper', in April 1982 it was 'scrap metal'. On March 19th that year a group of Argentine scrap metal merchants led by Senor Constantino Sergio Davidoff strode ashore at Leith on the island of South Georgia, a British dependency in the South Atlantic, some 8,000 miles from the British mainland. Their presence eventually led to Britain becoming embroiled in its first major conflict since the end of the Korean War.

BRITANNIA STANDS ALONE

By John Hughes-Wilson

Author and broadcaster Colonel John Hughes-Wilson, served as an Intelligence Officer in the Falklands after the Argentine surrender in June 1982.

In 1982, everyone knew that the era of Britain going to war on her own was a thing of the past. The very thought that a full-scale sea, air and land battle could be fought thousands of miles from home was almost unthinkable. The idea that television screens could be full of ships boiling with flame, aeroplanes tumbling from the sky with screaming pilots trapped inside them, and black faced infantrymen trying to rip each others bellies open with bayonets was just beyond belief. Things like that just didn't happen any more, or so the armchair pundits said.

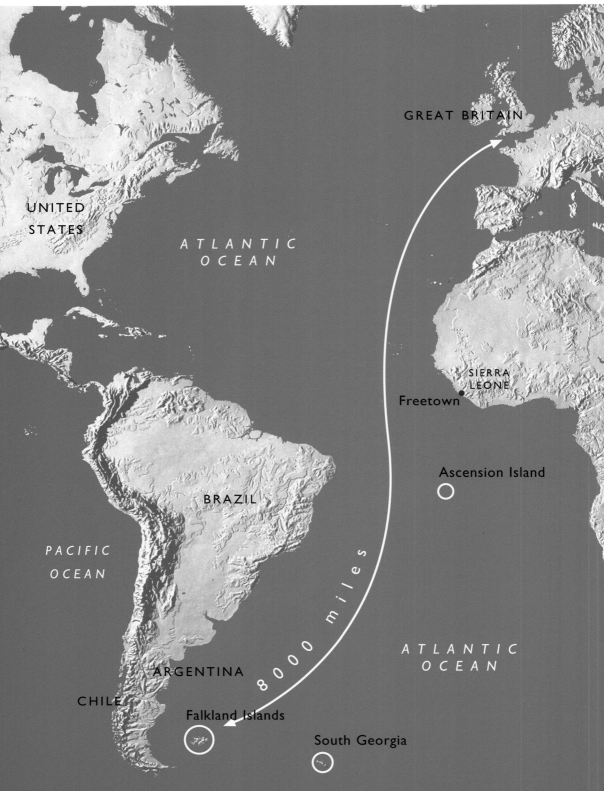

GREAT BRITAIN

UNITED
STATES

ATLANTIC
OCEAN

SIERRA
LEONE

Freetown

Ascension Island

BRAZIL

PACIFIC
OCEAN

8000 miles

ATLANTIC
OCEAN

ARGENTINA

CHILE

Falkland Islands

South Georgia

They were wrong in 1982 and, are probably wrong today. The Falklands war remains one of the defining moments of British post-colonial history. It showed once and for all that general war was not a thing of the past for western democracies. It showed that British politicians and the people still had the stomach to fight. Above all it showed that the British armed forces, although small, were a formidable foe. After 1982, nothing was quite the same again. A deeply unpopular Prime Minister went from being an insignificant politician to an almost totemic figurehead, prepared to stand and fight on any controversial issue.

The roots of the Falklands conflict ran deep and lay in the disputed ownership of a remote group of islands in the South Atlantic, four hundred miles from Argentina. They were first recorded by a Dutch navigator in 1600 and named by the British in 1690 in honour of Viscount Falkland, a navy minister.

The first settlers were actually French. In 1764 they built a fort, Port Louis, on East Falkland and called the group les Malouines after the islands off St Malo - hence the Spanish, 'los Malvinas'. A year later the British landed on West Falkland without even knowing that the French were holding the eastern island. It was a fine old eighteenth century colonial muddle, and was eventually solved by the British agreeing to give up their settlement and sail away after the French ceded the islands to their ally, Spain, in 1767. By 1790 all that remained of British presence was a bronze plaque.

'I tarry in this miserable desert suffering everything for the love of God.'

With the collapse of the Spanish empire the islands became derelict. In 1832 a US warship, the USS *Lexington*, cleared the Falkands / Malvinas of pirates and brigands and declared them 'free of all government.' Into this vacuum sailed the Royal Navy in 1837 with a battleship, declaring the Falkland Islands to be part of the British Crown's territories despite the government in Buenos Aires insisting that all the Spanish territories in the New World now belonged to the successor states - in this case, Argentina. The British - who had landed settlers - claimed that the tiny population of the islands was British and they stubbornly wished to remain so.

Anyone who has visited the islands cannot fail to be surprised by their remoteness and bleakness. In 1760 a Royal Marine (RM) officer said, 'I tarry in this miserable desert suffering everything for the love of God.' Two centuries later, in 1981, another RM officer described the islanders, or Kelpers as they call themselves, as 'a mainly drunken...and indolent collection of drop outs'. This was a harsh judgement. By 1982 the islanders were relying entirely on the British government and one single company, Coalite, for their economic survival. A British Trade Union MP even called them 'company slaves'. This small population - some 1,800 strong in 1982 - had only one unifying attribute: an understandable loyalty to the British Crown. From the point of view of Britain's Foreign and Commonwealth Office (FCO) this was a major irritant. A tiny handful of islanders were standing in the way of Britain's good relations with 28 million Argentines and 250 million South Americans.

For years the FCO's policy had been to divest itself of this colonial relic. Unfortunately for the world-weary bureaucrats of Whitehall, the Islanders thought differently. And the Islanders had a trump card. Under Article 73 of the UN Charter, the Falklanders were guaranteed the right to self-determination of government. Looking at the dubious politics of Argentina since 1945 it is hard to fault the Kelpers' choice.

For the wily bureaucrats of King Charles' Street this was just another intellectual challenge, the more so once the UN passed Resolution 2065 in 1965 calling on Britain and Argentina to find a negotiated settlement. For nearly twenty years the talks dragged on, the Argentines demanding, 'nuestras islas Malvinas', and the FCO trying to find more and more complex leaseback procedures to cede sovereignty to the Argentine without antagonising the stubborn Kelpers.

By 1981 the negotiations were in serious trouble on two fronts. In New York the talks were on the verge of breaking down in the presence of implacable Islanders' resistance. Even massive Argentine bribes of 'a million dollars a family' were allegedly rejected by the suspicious Kelpers who one source claims were insisting on 'a million dollars a head... but only for real Kelpers.'

The second fault line was the arrival of a new military Junta in Argentina in December 1981. Confronted by the aftermath of the 'dirty war' and the rising anger over 'los desaparecidos', the 'disappeared', General Galtieri's regime had to find a fast track to national unification. Like so many regimes before and since the Junta elected to use an external grievance to divert attention from domestic difficulties. Admiral Anaya, the Naval member of the Junta had a solution: reconquer the Malvinas. The Junta, facing rebellion on the streets, economic meltdown in the market place and with American assurances of 'standing together against communism in South America' saw an opportunity to boost their position and win popularity at home. Unfortunately they totally misjudged Britain's likely reaction.

Early in January 1982, Admiral Anaya's planning staff went to work on a secret operational plan to seize the islands. The strategic basis was to be a Goa-like operation, using naval operational assets to effect a swift *coup de main* that would evict the tiny British garrison and take the islands for Argentina. Once seized, at 8,000 miles range the islands were too far from UK to be recaptured, said the planners. It was to be a diplomatic, political and military fait accompli.

There were even hints from the British that such a solution would not be an unthinkable turn of events. After all, the Argentine diplomats pointed out, had

HMS Endurance, guardian of the Falkland Islands. British hints that she was to be decommissioned gave the Argentines confidence that they could occupy the Islands unhindered.

A171

Members of the Buzos Tacticos, shortly after the attack on the Royal Marine Garrison at Port Stanley.

not the British elected to dispose of HMS *Endurance*, the Falkland Islands guard ship? Had not the British Defence secretary, John Nott announced that the Royal Navy was to be run down, and the carriers sold off? All that remained, reasoned the Junta, was to test the British nerve.

South Georgia, a set of islands some 800 miles to the East, deep in the South Atlantic, became the litmus test of Whitehall's resolve. On 19th March 1982 Senor Constantino Davidoff led his forty scrap metal merchants ashore at Leith on South Georgia, ostensibly to fulfil an old contract to dismantle the rusting whaling station. As Senor Davidoff's team was transported in an Argentine naval auxiliary, the *Bahia Buen Suceso* and as they marched in step up the beach to salute the Argentinian flag which had been raised on one of the derelict buildings, few believed that they were peaceful civilians. Admiral Lombardo, Commander in Chief of the Argentine Atlantic Fleet was allegedly furious at this brazen provocation: but, as promised by his boss Admiral Anaya,

no friend of the British, the British government reacted timidly. On 22nd March the 'scrap team' re-embarked and it looked as if the crisis was over. In fact, Davidoff's scrap merchants had already lit the fuze of war for not all the Argentines had left South Georgia. A small team had stayed behind. Exasperated, the FCO ordered HMS *Endurance* to arrest them. Like some great chess game the Argentine navy promptly deployed war ships to 'protect their citizens'. Captain Nick Barker of *Endurance*, an old South Atlantic hand - who had reported to the Admiralty as early as 25th January that, 'the Argies were up to something' - wisely took to his heels and on 26th March began playing cat and mouse with three Argentine frigates deep in the watery wastes of the Southern Ocean. The clock was now ticking.

Astonishingly, the British government was still not ready for a war. Despite hard intelligence that the Argentine Navy's only carrier and submarines were at sea, despite reports that aircraft were on alert, that a Marine battalion was embarked and a SEAL team headed for Port Stanley, Whitehall's Latin American Current Intelligence Group - led by the ever-emollient FCO - blithely advised the Prime Minister that the Argentines were only sabre rattling and that 'no invasion was imminent'. It was a breathtaking miscalculation.

On 2nd April 1982, Commandos of the Argentine Marine Infantry supported by special forces of the *Buzo Tactico* poured ashore at Port Stanley shortly after 6.00 a.m. and after a brief skirmish captured the tiny Royal Marine garrison who were outnumbered ten to one and without any fire support. The Falkland Islands Governor, Sir Rex Hunt, formally surrendered Government House at 9.30 a.m. The images of the surrendered British Royal Marines, face down in the dirt with Argentine rifles held by black balaclava clad Argentine Commandos pointing at them, sent shock waves round the world and shook the foundations of the Palace of Westminster.

But it was not just the British who had miscalculated. Faced by an angry House of Commons baying for blood, Prime Minister Thatcher did the only thing she could to ensure her government's survival. Buoyed up by the counsel of the First Sea Lord, Sir Henry Leach - who, cynics said, seized a chance to save his beloved Navy from John Nott's defence cuts - Thatcher elected to make a fight of it. Within a week a Task Force had sailed, with orders to regain the Falklands for the British Crown, by force if necessary. Operation Corporate was underway.

Scenes that shook Westminster. Face down in the dirt, Royal Marines are searched after the surrender of Government House.

THE TASK FORCE

Three days after the Argentine capture of Port Stanley the first ships of the British Task Force - the aircraft carriers *Hermes* and *Invincible* - sailed from Portsmouth against a background of frenetic diplomatic activity. Initially the Task Force was a primarily naval effort, cobbled together without any real staff appreciation of the force levels and resources required to complete the mission. At this stage, no one actually envisaged a real shooting war. The swift - and undoubtedly rushed - departure of the carriers was dictated more by symbolism than reality. The message intended for Buenos Aires, and also at Britain's array of protagonists vying for a place at the top table of international relations, was clear. Britain would respond and respond forcefully. Britannia was brandishing her trident.

Within a week of the high visibility departure of the aircraft carriers, the first units of the land based element of the Task Force sailed from Southampton. Naval and air power were essential to the mission but barring a diplomatic settlement

Soldiers of the Argentine invasion force pose for the camera. John Hughes-Wilson

or an Argentine withdrawal the British would eventually have to get 'boots ashore' in order to retake and clear the Islands. That would necessitate an amphibious assault the like of which had not been attempted by Britain - acting alone - since the Second World War. Given the nature of the task ahead, 3 Commando Brigade Royal Marines, (40, 42 and 45 Commandos) under Brigadier Julian Thompson were at the core of the land element. The 2nd Battalion of the Parachute Regiment, (2 Para) then on five days notice to move and its sister unit the 3rd Battalion (3 Para), then acting as 'Spearhead' and ready for immediate deployment, were extracted from the newly formed 5 Brigade and attached to 3 Commando Brigade. These

The British Task Force sets sail from Portsmouth to retake the Falklands.

five units, along with the Special Air Service (SAS) and Special Boat Squadron (SBS) were, in 1982, probably the most highly trained, efficient and physically conditioned troops in the British Army. Their reputation as tough, professional, highly motivated and experienced soldiers - the units had all seen active service in Northern Ireland - was recognised and respected worldwide.

3 Para and most of 3 Commando Brigade sailed from Southampton on board the 45,000 ton requisitioned cruise liner S.S. *Canberra* on Good Friday 9th April amidst emotional scenes on the quaysides not witnessed for decades.

DOWN SOUTH ON THE 'GREAT WHITE WHALE'
By Nick Rose

Nick Rose was a twenty year-old private in B Company, 3 Para in April 1982. Here he recalls the events surrounding the news of the Argentine invasion and the voyage to war.

We were on notice as the 'Spearhead' battalion. There was always one Para battalion on 'Spearhead' - ready to go at short notice. I was on extra duties. I don't know what I'd done wrong but I was given 'extras' in the Sergeants' Mess, doing the dixies. A real dick job. I had extras the week before and I hadn't been home for more than three weeks. That was the deal. We near Andover, so me and some of the 'Barnardo's Boys' - the blokes who hadn't really got a home to go to - went out on the piss and started getting caned. Especially when they said we'd be confined to camp.

I think rumour started which said you'd best go and look at detail - special detail, daily orders amendment. 'Khandahar', that was the code word I think - bringing everybody back that went out to the railway stations. It was '3 Para Khandahar' and that was the recall word. We were on 'spearhead', which was why we had a recall word. I can't remember who told me but it was word of mouth with blokes saying - 'F***** H***, we're going to the Falklands'.

All we heard was that Argentina had invaded South Georgia and the Falklands and some blokes were going, 'where the **** are the Falklands. Are they in Scotland?' It was like that. The Shetlands? The Falklands? For a simple 'squaddie' there's no great need for them to have a knowledge of world geography. I'm not slating the blokes at all but they'd probably sooner go and have a drink. Then I thought hang on where are they? We got an intelligence briefing, probably the day after. This was when it really had 'hit the fan' and the button had been pushed - we were definitely going. It was decision made there and then upstairs at Number 10 and Northwood because the turnaround time from when the Argentines first landed in South Georgia and the Falklands was quick. We were down there within eight weeks, which is pretty good going.

You must bear in mind the average age [of the paras]. I was 20. I didn't really know if it was 'Monday or the zoo'. I was naive in many ways of the world but I'd been well trained to do my job. I'd been to Ireland so I'd had experience of carrying loaded weapons and their potential and I'd 'savvied' up professionally. Everyone was like, 'Well OK but we've got to do it'. That's what you had to say. If it comes to doing it you've got to do it. But the further south we got and because the peace process was going on - they were really going for it - in a way everyone was hoping that well, maybe they'd cancel it. And this is when people started to think, 'look at us' and you look at the situation you're in, sitting on a massive cruise liner in the middle of the South Atlantic Ocean, sailing off 8,000 miles to fight an enemy that outnumbers you by x, y, z to one, firmly dug in and entrenched in perfect defensive positions. If it had been us defending those mountains no one would have been going anywhere. They would not have got past - would not have got through to Stanley - at least not via the mountains. Perfect defensive positions. So I was scared but I was excited with the adrenalin. There were some very intelligent people around and as we sailed on we used to sit and chat and after a while we'd think, 'it really is going to happen. We really are going to war', so I was scared and I was excited but I was caught up in the belief that we'd have to do it so let's just get on with it and do the best we can. I think that was the general consensus. I am sure the overwhelming majority would say the same.

Some people called the *Canberra* 'The Great White Whale' but we just used to call it 'the boat' which used to piss the Marines off. Ships carry boats! We had the greatest respect for each other but we used to call them 'cabbage heads, 'leathernecks' and things like that. They called us 'cherry berets'.

The first week was just chaos. There was stuff on the ship that shouldn't have been where it was and it had to be moved elsewhere. There were tons and tons of ammunition and food to be moved. The logistics were unbelievable. It took a couple of days but they squared it.

Task Force South. Private Nick Rose on the deck of the Canberra off Freetown harbour, Sierra Leone May 7th 1982. Note the training shoes. The Paras were not allowed to wear boots on deck. Nick Rose

There were four men in a four-man room - each man had his own bed. In a two-man room - like the one Stew Grey had - he had a water tap - water that you could drink and it was comfy enough. After the first week we established a pattern. Obviously ship's husbandry - that's what they called it - the washing up, the cleaning, still had to be done. The *Canberra* had lost a lot of staff who'd done all these jobs, so we were given jobs. I used to work in the laundry. Me and my pals had the best pressed kit on the ship. I used to wear baggy OG's [olive greens] issued around the time of the Suez crisis I think. You had to be a bit of an old sweat to wear them but by that time I was a bit of a sweat because I had a 'badge', I'd been to Ireland.

Up at 7.00 a.m., queue up for your scoff at various times - A Company at 7.00, B Company at 7.15 - so that's 120 men, the full complement of a company with all its supporting arms. But you got through. 8 o'clock was muster. What to wear? Get your trainers on and your sweat top on and it was 'bang, bang, bang' round the promenade deck - a quarter of a mile each time. You used to get platoons of blokes just going 'bump, bump, bump bump', and the ship used to shake and vibrate. We could feel it when the Marines were doing their turn because it was the Para Regiment at x, y, z time and the Marines at another time. Sub units would be practising all over the ship. On the forward deck the anti-tank platoon would be doing demos on the Milan and the Wombat with the GPMGs doing their bit on the 'forward, sub aft deck of the overhead underhang!' But we eventually found our way around.

It was an emphasis on weapons familiarisation. Just going back over and over and over things - a sensible move - with a lot of fitness thrown in. That was the main thing, sensible fitness, and a lot of admin'- getting yourself squared up.

We got briefs about possible ways of going in the nearer we got. We knew we were not going to be airlifted in and that there was going to be an amphibious landing. I think this was established on day one at Northwood or somewhere else that the actual assault was going to be via landing craft from HMS *Fearless* and *Intrepid* and that some of the people who were going to be doing it would be the Parachute

3 Para lifejacket drill on Ascension Island. Left to right: Private Nick Rose, Private Harry Gannon, Private Steve Holland, Private Pete Partridge. Nick Rose

Regiment - the 3rd Battalion - so better get some training in on cross-decking at Ascension Island.

We berthed at Ascension Island and I was on the *Intrepid*. We were practising with their LCU's (Landing Craft Utility). An LCU holds a platoon, the front goes down and its 'charge'. So we were practising getting in off the side of the *Canberra* and if you look at the *Canberra* its a huge great thing. Ten foot above the water line there's a big door - 10 foot high by 8 wide - which was one of the loading doors - an area where you can store stuff but obviously blokes can gather there as opposed to stores. This is where we learned how to get on this LCU and you've got to time it correctly because of the swell - massive ship, small ship - it's not rocket science. If you time it wrong 'bang' you're in there. Someone fell in between the ship and an LCU-he bust his hip or his pelvis - and the urban myth grew that he had been attacked by trigger fish - like sea piranhas. We used to catch them in our 'cam' nets, beat them up and throw them back in and watch the feeding frenzy that followed.

And then you start getting company briefs and later start getting ammunition issued - 'divvying' up the 'link' for the 'Gimpys' [GPMGs - General Purpose Machine Guns] - that man's got the '66s' and you're given two mortars to carry onto the landing beach from the LCU. That's when you finally think to yourself 'this is a 'go'.

Denuded of 2 and 3 Para, 5 Infantry Brigade, consisting solely of 1st / 7th Gurkha Rifles, was made up to strength with the addition of the 1st Battalion the Welsh Guards and the 2nd Battalion of the Scots Guards fresh from ceremonial duties at Windsor Castle and Buckingham Palace. 5 Brigade was considered an ad hoc formation, designed initially as a reinforcing garrison unit once 3 Commando Brigade had done their job. As the Task Force sailed south from Ascension Island however, and diplomacy trickled into the sand, a grimmer reality emerged and as that reality set in, so the Task Force began to look woefully inadequate for the job at hand. For a start, with only 36 Harriers, there were too few planes. At no

B Company, 3 Para, pose for a group photograph during the voyage 'down south'. Nick Rose

Crippled. HMS Sheffield *falls victim to the first successful Argentine Exocet attack.*

time did Rear Admiral Woodward, Commander of the Carrier Battle Group, have anything like total air superiority. With his two carriers acting as the Task Force's only airfields, Woodward prudently kept them well to the East, earning the derisive comment from some wag that he deserved the 'East Africa Star' not the South Atlantic Medal at the war's end. However, he was, like Jellicoe at Jutland, 'the only man who could have lost the war in an afternoon.' Unlike Jellicoe, Woodward won.

The Task Force was finally committed to battle on 1st May 1982, following the failure of the US Secretary of State Al Haig's diplomatic efforts to get the Argentines off of the islands. The British slapped a 200 mile Total Exclusion Zone (TEZ) around the Falklands and flew an astonishing Vulcan bomber mission - with no less than seventeen air to air refuellings - from Ascension to crater the runway at Stanley. It failed but the war had started in earnest. If the Argentines wouldn't leave voluntarily, then Whitehall would blockade them on their ill-gotten gains.

Blow followed blow in quick succession. On 2nd May the elderly cruiser General Belgrano, which in a previous incarnation as the USS *Phoenix*, had escaped destruction by the Japanese at Pearl Harbor, was sunk by a British nuclear submarine HMS *Conqueror*, effectively closing off the southern prong of the Argentine Navy's pincer attack on the Task Force. In the north, the carrier *Veinticinco de Mayo*, fled back to harbour. Whatever else, the Royal Navy's nuclear submarines had secured supremacy at sea.

There only remained the air threat; and on 4th May two land-based Mirages riposted with the first successful Exocet attack, crippling HMS *Sheffield*. The shock wave reverberated throughout the Royal Navy. Suddenly the Task Force looked very vulnerable indeed. Years of Treasury penny pinching and cost cutting suddenly looked like risking every ship afloat, as fire boiled through *Sheffield*'s flimsy hull feeding off cheap plastic electrical trunking and melting sailors' acrylic trousers into their very flesh.

For the next two weeks the Navy's tactics changed to a series of night bombardments designed to put pressure on Argentine positions ashore. At dawn the Task Force would make a rapid withdrawal to the East to re-supply at sea and

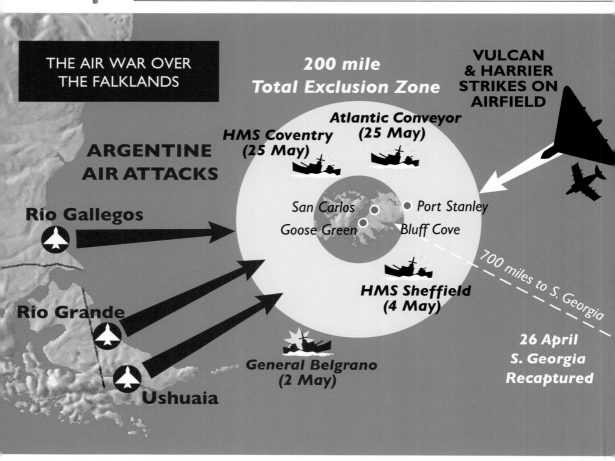

THE AIR WAR OVER THE FALKLANDS

200 mile Total Exclusion Zone

VULCAN & HARRIER STRIKES ON AIRFIELD

Atlantic Conveyor (25 May)

HMS Coventry (25 May)

ARGENTINE AIR ATTACKS

San Carlos
Goose Green

Port Stanley
Bluff Cove

Rio Gallegos

700 miles to S. Georgia

HMS Sheffield (4 May)

Rio Grande

26 April S. Georgia Recaptured

General Belgrano (2 May)

Ushuaia

continue the nerve-wracking lookout for the next Argentine air attacks. Time was not on the Task Force's side. The steady loss of key ships, particularly the Type 42 destroyers, sapped the nerves of the crews and the crippling lack of any early warning radar meant that the ships were always vulnerable to air attack. The truth was that as a strategic deployment to create the conditions for an amphibious landing, the Task Force had achieved little. The Commando Brigade and the rest of General Jeremy Moore's soldiers were not ashore, and the Argentine Air Force still remained, formidable and dangerous.

THE LANDING

Ⅰn London, at Joint Headquarters Northwood and afloat in HMS *Hermes*, the war planners' options were running out. The British needed a new war strategy, and fast. As the Navy's demonstration of force had failed to frighten the Argentines off the islands, it seemed that only a full-blooded amphibious assault and land battle could clinch a decisive victory. On 21st May - D-Day - the British forces went ashore at Port San Carlos, San Carlos and Ajax Bay on East Falkland in what was, with hindsight, an extraordinarily bold, three phase operation. Brigadier Thompson's 'design' for battle involved a silent attack by landing craft during the hours of darkness with all high ground being secured by dawn.

3 Para were to be 'cross decked' from the *Canberra* to the assault ship *Intrepid* and landed near Sand Bay and Port San Carlos - codenamed Green Beaches One and Two - by landing craft during the second phase of the operation to secure Port San Carlos to the north. Led by B Company, whose task was to secure the beach itself, the rest of the battalion were then to push through and dig in on the reverse slopes of the high ground at Windy Gap and Settlement Rocks to secure

A. Assault ships Intrepid *and* Fearless *move into position. Troops transferred to Landing Craft.* B. *3 SBS dropped by helicopter and attack Argentine unit on Fanning Head.* C. *Troops land and push on to secure high ground.* D. *Argentine Combat Team 'Eagle' shoot down two Gazelle helicopters as they retreat from Port San Carlos.*

the beachhead. Scimitar and Scorpion Light tanks of 4 Troop, the Blues and Royals were to accompany them to soften up any Argentine resistance. If everything had gone according to plan all 671 men of 3 Para, including a forty man attachment of 9 (Parachute) Squadron RE, would have been loaded onto the landing craft by 4.15 a.m. and ashore by 6.05 a.m. but the first wave landings were delayed. With first light at around 6.30 local time, this meant that 3 Para would now go ashore at around 7.30 a.m. in daylight. Australian director Peter Weir's film 'Gallipoli', had already been screened on the voyage south and in order to counteract any complacency on the part of his men, Lieutenant Colonel Hew Pike, their commanding officer, had

> **'Do not be daunted if chaos reigns, because it undoubtedly will.'**

already warned that the landing might have more than a whiff of the ill-fated assault on the beaches of Gallipoli 67 years earlier. He also came on the *Intrepid*'s 'pipes' and paraphrased the words of Brigadier James Hill, Commander of 3 Parachute Brigade, who had addressed his men on the eve of the Normandy landings in June 1944: 'Do not be daunted if chaos reigns, because it undoubtedly will.' [1]

As the convoy of assault ships nosed into San Carlos Water the sound of a firefight could be heard off to their left from the direction of high ground of Fanning Head accompanied by naval gunfire support from HMS *Antrim*. Here a patrol of 3 SBS, which had been airlifted ashore earlier, were engaging an Argentine combat team known as 'The Fanning Head Mob' in order to secure the approaches to San Carlos Water. Another Argentine combat team - 'Eagle' - were also in the area of Port San Carlos, and although in the event the landings were unopposed as the Argentines withdrew to the north, the small force of 41 men could have caused mayhem on Green Beach. This point was demonstrated to lethal effect after the landings as that same Argentine combat team, moving away from Port San Carlos, fired on and brought down two Gazelle helicopters and damaged a third. Three crewmen died. [2]

3 Para get 'boots on the beach' at Port San Carlos after an 8,000 mile journey. At this point they are most vunerable to Argentine attack.

3 Para RSM Lawrie Ashbridge, is received with a warm cup of tea and an even warmer welcome by members of the Ford and Summers families at Port San Carlos. Tom Smith, Daily Express

At this point the landings were at their most vulnerable from air strikes but after an uncomfortable and nerve wracking run in, which seemed to take an age, the bow ramps of most of the landing craft crunched down onto the beach. 3 Para were ashore at last. But as 3 Para dug in their troubles were only just beginning. Eight thousand miles from home, with limited logistic and ammunition stocks and without air superiority the assault from the sea was at risk from the moment it was launched. Most of all it was at risk from the air.

The Argentine counterattack was swift in coming. Flying at suicidally low altitudes to attack the targets anchored in the sound, the Argentine pilots hurled themselves against the ships offshore. Despite a blizzard of anti-aircraft fire the young pilots pushed home their attacks with great bravery. Many were shot down, but to the British soldiers ashore trying to build up their positions, the vital shipping in San Carlos Water seemed to be being badly mauled.

HITTING THE BEACH
Ashore at Port San Carlos - D-Day 21st May 1982
By Nick Rose

We'd got a standing platoon in the landing craft I'd say. This was supposed to be a night landing. Major problems somewhere along the line and by the time we'd jumped on to these little boats it was daylight. Great news! This is supposed to be a night assault and we had no direct support as such. As we started to turn to go in there was a big firefight going on at Fanning Head - Special Forces guys taking on these forward recce' Argies. From the intelligence that filtered back we thought the landing would be unopposed. That's why Special Forces were over there. If they hadn't taken on those guys on Fanning Head then it would have been an opposed landing. But then would it? The Argentines were forward recce' guys and they wouldn't have wanted to engage a battalion sized assault as a small platoon, or 20 man, section strength fighting patrol. Good job Special Forces took them out though. They saw them off and then we went in but it was broad daylight and it was, 'Oh God' because there was air raid warning 'red' all the time. They'd tried it before and they were going to try it again soon. It was a serious situation and then to get wet boots and freezing nuts on top of it.

When we actually came to do it for real the front of our landing craft wouldn't go down so we went over the side. There's two marines, one on either side at the top of the landing craft with two GPMGs going 'get the fuck out of here.' Not a great start - wet boots and freezing nuts! We were only about four or five feet out but it was up to your nuts.

I was carrying my bergen with everything you need for three or four days - cold weather kit, ammunition - when we went in we probably had 500 rounds linked for the guns - and each man had a mortar tube - 81mm SLR [self-loading rifle], webbing stuffed with ammunition, water, survival kit. You wanted to carry as much as you possibly could.

There have been vast exaggerations about the weight carried - honestly some of the claims would be just physically impossible to do - but on average each man was carrying 140 lbs, which is a ten stone man. O.K. it's distributed across your shoulders because it's designed that way and it's a very good way of carrying a lot of weight for a long time. Webbing likewise if you've got it correctly fitted. I used to sew my water bottle pouches together - sew it up with fishing line - so there was no 'jacking' around, padded it out on the inside, then' cam'd' it all up. The blokes who 'savvied' up were a lot more comfortable than the guys who didn't. You've got to pack a bergen correctly as well. If you went down on your back you had to be pulled up by another bloke, you had to, you could not physically do it yourself. You were just like a tortoise on its back.

We all had pre-designated areas at Port San Carlos so there was a lot of talking about the landing and a lot of orders. This is happening - now we are going to war. We are going to close with and destroy the enemy, no messing about. The Special Forces guys were over there and patrols had been in the night before and had marked out where we were going to go with a markalite path. Then we advanced up to the top of this bare-arsed, featureless hill - horrible - but we had to get up there because you've got your view and you can see quite some way. 'Bang', get in there - dig in - get yourself squared up. Dig in - that was it and that was a nightmare because it was bog where we were. You dug down a foot and you hit water so the idea was to try and build your position up a bit and pack the bottom of your 'hole' with moss and heather. We were on the reverse slopes at Windy Ridge. We tried to establish a routine, we couldn't advance too far because we were waiting on others to come in.

Then the aircraft started coming in and that's quite scary. Every ten minutes you'd get, aircraft warning 'red' or air raid warning 'red' because we had Rapier [surface to air missiles] and the climate down there does not lend itself to sensitive equipment

A soldier from the Parachute Regiment in full battle dress. The Paras had to carry heavy bergens weighing up to 140lb containing everything they needed to survive and fight in extreme weather conditions.

Illustrated by Jon Wilkinson

27

The Rapier (surface to air missile) in action. The weather played havoc with its sensitive electronics making it prone to give off false air raid alarms. Although a potential life saver, this tended to make the troops complacent.

as was the Rapier then, electronically speaking - a lot of the stuff is now obsolete and the electronics can be duplicated on something the size of your watch but the Rapier was a great big thing. I'm not slagging it off - if it helps save my life, thank you very much - but it was very sensitive. So every ten minutes the alarm would go off on the Rapier and we'd stand to and people just became complacent. Like crying wolf. But there was a part of me which was always wary. On occasions these Skyhawks would come over and its quite shocking because wherever you are, when you look at one, it looks as if it's coming directly at you. It's something of an optical illusion, albeit it's 200 - 300 feet above you. It's going about 5-600 m.p.h. and its just loosed off a load of 'shit' at the boats in the Sound - that's quite a scary thing but then, 'da-da-da-da- da' blokes are having some, despite being specifically told, 'do not engage aircraft with small arms fire', because - well, there's blokes over here, blokes over there, blokes everywhere - there was the risk of hitting your own blokes. But everyone starts 'lamming' it up there.

There was a guy with a GPMG and he gave it 'the max' from the hip. Mark Hamill - a big bloke was Mark, a PTI and a very hard but a very fair man - a good soldier - was on a Milan and he fired at a Skyhawk and missed it. Now there's £10,000 every time you fire one of those down the range. So Hamill just fired this and he missed the aircraft. Can you imagine? He got a major bollocking but imagine if he'd hit it? - Victoria Cross, 'well done'. So yes we'd give it some rattle when these things came over but it was very scary, because we did feel we'd lost momentum. I'm sure word was coming down from Brigadier Thompson or whoever to start pushing on. We had to start moving on. It just felt that we'd been there a while. The Argentines knew we were in this position, they knew where we were displaced so it did feel we'd been there too long. So let's get on and start the advance.

As with so many air battles however, the decisive fighting was taking place well away from the surface observers and in reality RAF and RN Harrier pilots were catching many of the Argentine attackers both inbound and outbound from their bombing runs on the ships. The Harrier, like its feathered namesake, was turning out to be a deadly close quarters aerial killer. The British pilots were using new American Sidewinder missiles, - although one pilot shot down a Skyhawk with his cannons at a range of less than 100 yards - and the air kills ratio was firmly in the British favour. By the end of the first day the Argentines had lost 16 attacking aircraft: an unsustainable loss. For the next three days the air assault continued, but slowly ebbed away. By 25th May there was even talk of having 'beaten the air threat'.

All that changed on 25th May, Argentina's National Day. At first, the British thought that they had defeated the early waves of attacking aircraft. Then the Argentine pilots delivered a decisive and crippling double blow to the Task Force, sinking another Type 42, HMS *Coventry*, and, much more ominously, the most important supply ship afloat, the 13,000 ton *Atlantic Conveyor*, which went down, taking with it ten Wessex and three Chinook helicopters. Brigadier Thompson would later record the 25th as 'a black day.' The British strategy was now in serious jeopardy and from that most serious of military factors: logistics.

The war now became a race against time. In London enormous pressure was put on the commanders ashore to 'do something'. Fears of a UN imposed cease fire with the Task Force still sitting on the beach head, and public clamour for results after

Royal Navy Sea Harriers on patrol. The Harriers were the saviours of many ships as they intercepted Argentine airfcraft bent on inflicting damage to the Task Force.

the Navy's heavy shipping losses, forced Brigadier Thompson, and his commander, Jeremy Moore - against all their instincts and training - to embark on a series of rushed and poorly supported ground operations. This entailed 2 Para being ordered to attack the Argentine defenders of Darwin-Goose Green while the rest of his force embarked on the first stage of the 'investment' of the capital Port Stanley on the other side of the island. The breakout would soon be under way. With the loss of most of his helicopter transport Thompson's original plan to airlift the majority of his brigade forward was now in tatters. There was now only one way to get 3 Brigade forward and for 3 Para that would mean 'tabbing' it - walking every step of the way. Even so they were more than ready for a change of scene. Graham Colbeck, a Sergeant in the Milan anti-tank platoon, concluded his diary entry for 26th May with a sentence which summed up the feelings of his comrades. 'Everyone here just wants to get to Stanley and finish it off.'[3]

THE 'TAB'

The order to move out of the Port San Carlos beach head came on 27th May. It was D + 6. Instead of waiting for the arrival of 5 Brigade as they had expected, 3 Para were now told to advance and capture Teal Inlet, a settlement some 25 miles east of their present positions. This area had been earmarked as a forward logistics base for the final phase of operations to capture Port Stanley and had already been reconnoitred by the SBS. The axis of the advance chosen by Brigadier Thompson lay north of the spine of high ground that ran across East Falkland from San Carlos Water in the west almost to the outskirts of Stanley in the east. 2 Para had already moved out from their beach head on the other side of San Carlos Water on the first leg of their fateful journey to Goose Green and now it was 3 Para's turn.

THE 'TAB' ACROSS EAST FALKLAND 27th - 31st MAY 1982

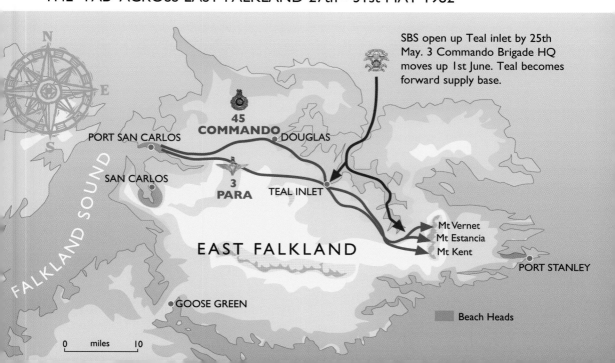

Shortly after dawn, 45 Commando set out to 'yomp' - heavily laden with all their kit like pack animals - along a recognised track to Douglas settlement via New House, followed shortly afterwards by 3 Para who were to 'tab', in 'light order' - no bergens, no sleeping bags, no tripods for the sustained fire role GPMGs - in their wake as far as Douglas, before passing through to take the lead. Lieutenant Colonel Pike, had, however, discussed the route to Teal with Mr. Alan Miller, the civilian manager of the Port San Carlos settlement and had learned of a more direct route, albeit not using recognised tracks. The mortar section also hitched a lift on Mr. Miller's two tractors, one of them driven by his son Philip. Even so, they would have to rely on the now tenuous logistics support to 'chopper' their kit forward to pre-arranged locations.[1] And so it fell to 3 Para to blaze the trail. The march was a supreme test of 3 Para's physical and mental stamina across more than twenty miles, in just two stages, of some of the most featureless and spirit-sapping terrain, in what some men could only described as 'bizarre' climatic conditions. Men called on inner reserves of personal pride and networks of mutual support: they drew heavily from the well of their tough training regime and regimental *esprit de corps* as the weather threw everything at them over mile after endless mile of stumbling over tussocks of pale grass and foot snagging heather. The 'tab' was no respecter of previous achievement. Men seen as some of the fittest in the battalion, due to their scores in the British Army's conditioning tests, became exhausted and there were several who turned their ankles as sodden socks slid around in the universally loathed and equally soaked DMS [direct moulded sole] ankle boots. Trench foot, a condition well known to the men of the British Army of 14 -18, now beckoned to these men of '82. [2]

The battalion reached its objective on 29th May, secured it and stayed there for twenty-four hours before embarking on the next stage of their odyssey on 30th May. The objective was Estancia House, a tiny settlement consisting of the eponymous house itself, a barn and a few outbuildings that were reached on the night of 31st May/1st June. Intelligence had warned of up to 300 Argentine troops in the area but by the time 3 Para arrived they had disappeared towards Stanley. Several Argentine prisoners were picked up on the way as 3 Para finally caught up with stragglers from Combat Team Eagle who had withdrawn from the area of Port San Carlos on D - Day. Also picked up on the way, and a most welcome addition to the ranks of 3 Para, was Terry Peck, the former Falkland Islands Chief Police Officer, member of the Falkland Islands Defence Force and member of its Legislative Council, vehemently opposed to any moves legitimising Argentine sovereignty over the Islands. Peck had already witnessed one Argentine invasion of sorts, when, in September, 1966, a civilian Dakota airliner was hijacked by armed Peronist youths over Patagonia and landed on Stanley racecourse. As Chief Police Officer Peck became involved and at one point had a gun pointed in his direction. Now, during this invasion he had determined not to remain impotent in Stanley as the Argentines swarmed around town and so escaped on a motorbike. Riding west he eventually made contact with elements of 3 Para left behind at Port San Carlos after the rest of the battalion had set off for Teal Inlet. Airlifted forward he became an honorary member of D Patrol Company, whose members used his intimate knowledge of East Falkland's geography to their advantage in the days ahead.

The importance of securing Estancia House and the high ground of Mounts Estancia - (occupied by A Company) and Vernet (C and elements of B Company) which lay to the north east, was essential in building a seven mile long, north - south platform of high ground - a platform which included the strategically valuable and already occupied heights of Mount Kent - from which 3 Commando Brigade could launch the assault on the outer ring of the Stanley defences. The Estancia position itself was situated on the shore of one of the fingers of several inlets, which branched off southeast from Teal and which pointed towards Stanley, now only 15 miles away as the shell flies. It was essential as it reduced the supply line from San Carlos by almost a fifth, as a round trip from Teal to 3 Para's area of operations was now only 15 miles as opposed to 100 from San Carlos. In addition, the Estancia/Vernet position was vital in anchoring the northern axis of Brigadier Thompson's plan for a two-pronged 'investment of Stanley'. Its importance was further enhanced as the Argentine commander Menendez became ever more convinced - particularly after 2 Para's victory at Goose Green - that the eventual British assault would be unleashed along the Fitzroy - Stanley track to the south. [3]

> **All you're thinking of is 'I'm carrying a 10 stone man on my back,**

The first snows of the South Atlantic winter fell on 1st June and in the momentary lulls between bouts of bad weather and poor visibility, 3 Para observers on the higher ground caught glimpses of Stanley a tantalising fifteen miles to the east and first set eyes on a feature bristling with jagged outcrops of rock jutting out at a crazy angle and rising to just under 500 feet high and about 500 yards across. It barred the way to Stanley and dominated the northern claw of Thompson's pincer as far back as the Estancia position and even to Teal Inlet beyond. Looking at the map 3 Para checked its name. Mount Longdon.

'DRY FAG, WARM BOOTS AND A CHEESE AND ONION SANDWICH.'
Memories of the 'Tab' across East Falkland
By Nick Rose

The march was a nightmare. This was our planned route to Stanley. I know it was supposed to be something like 60 kilometres but somebody 'guesstimated' that we probably did about 400 because we were doing a lot of forward patrols - not just D Patrol Company. You've got to dominate the ground so you have to have fighting patrols. Going cross-country was the worst terrain in the world. It was that clumpy moss and grass. People are falling down and ankles are going and once you're down on your back you've got to wait for the next guy to come up to help. And it is a tactical advance. 'Tabbing' is a name that comes from the letters TAB - Tactical Advance to Battle, - and we tabbed and carried everything with us. It may be that you have arrowhead

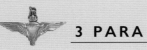

On the 'TAB'. Nick Rose's best friend, Tony 'Fester' Greenwood brews up under their 'basha'. Note the large boulders of the stone run behind them; a feature which helped to make the march extremely difficult. Nick Rose

6 platoon B Company dig in and take a break. Left to right: Corporal 'Granny' Paterson, Private Den Dunn, Private Tony Greenwood and **Nick Rose.** Nick Rose

formation going across, we had extended formation. We had picketing with guys on the high ground to either side. The terrain dictated exactly how we advanced. A lot of the time if we're going along on tracks - what few tracks we did go on - we used Indian file, which is staggered file on either side of the track, like a zig-zag. But there are great rivers of rocks [stone runs] - big white boulders - and you have to cross them and then there's the heather and the gorse and its constantly wet. So the wind chill factor was - I think somebody said - 40° - and storm force winds and horizontal rain - a nightmare scenario. People got sunburn one day - no air pollution - bizarre! It was a terrible advance - a mind numbing, bone-jarring advance. What do people think of? It was just head down, thumb up your bum, mind in neutral and 'go'. You've got to carry it. All you're thinking of is 'I'm carrying a 10 stone man on my back, I'm carrying a 10 stone man on my back'. Some of the guys, like the anti-tank or probably the mortars hitched lifts. They're 'blaggers' but fair play to them, there's no way you can lump base plates and that over that terrain. Even the GPMG guys in a sustained fire role - with the tripods.

There were some Scimitars and Scorpions with us. Once we were doing an advance or a recce' patrol and we were coming back on a track. We were Indian file - remember, we're still tactical paras, we're switched on - and this Scimitar pulls up and it's the bloke in charge. We are all horrible, we're miserable as sin, all of us -

Lord Robin Innes Kerr (right) and crew aboard their Scimitar.

we're missing home, want a dry fag, warm, dry boots, a cheese and onion sandwich and a bottle of blue top milk. I used to dream of these. Anyhow this bloke pulls up and pops out, 'what, what', and says would you like a lift. Oh yes please! So eight of us jump on and there are these vents at the front of the Scorpions and Scimitars blowing out hot air and we all just sat on there and we literally dried out. This bloke took pity on us and got his lads to make us a brew, because the Scorpions and Scimitars carry a massive boiler and they've always got constant hot water. It was no odds to him to give us some to make a cup of tea. He said he'd give us a lift back a little way. Turns out his name was the Lord Robin Innes Kerr. A genuine, nice bloke. I'd like to thank him for that. What a lovely gesture. I remember another thing - literally a lifesaver - on the other side of the Murrell River. It was a guy called Lawrie Ashbridge, the RSM, who sanctioned it. We were advancing in the dark and had been marching for 24 hours, we had to get up to the start line, or the preparation for moving on to the final start line - the FUP [Forming Up Position] - we were soaking wet and this was the most inhospitable weather we'd had since we'd been there. It was a nightmare - 'tramp', 'tramp' - blokes just moving inches at a time but an entire long snake of blokes doing exactly the same. You can imagine the speed of advance was minimal and the weather was horrible so Lawrie Ashbridge made a decision and told us to get into the side of the road - because we were still tactical, this was night time - get down by the side of the track, find as much cover as you can, get your ponchos out and get a brew on. So every man just got down, poncho out and brewed up. That, I am sure, saved people's lives, I'm sure of it. As a morale booster it was the best thing he could have done. If they are going to see us it doesn't matter if they smell us as well. So blokes are having a fag under their armpits. But such a simple thing as that can change the fortunes of war, or battles anyway. This was at the stage just before where we went across [the Murrell River] and started the advance. Perhaps two days before the battle.

On one occasion we were on a LRRP-Long Range Recconnaisance Patrol, just four men watching - supposed to be relieved after 24 hours. We were out there for two days. We'd got no food so we were eating our sugar - sachets of sugar - dried milk, scrabbling around desperately trying to find something to eat.

We were then told to stop. We'd advanced too far which is all very 'gung ho'. This was on the way in to the final destination. We were told to 'go firm' because the Marines couldn't keep up. I'm not saying that because the Marines are wankers because they're not - far from it - but I think they had a logistical problem so they couldn't advance and if we'd have carried on at the pace of advance that we were doing, our only option would have been to attack - just carry on going, just roll. But we were so over extended - we had no artillery support at that time - so I think Hew Pike got a bit of a bollocking for being a bit naughty but I think it had just got to the stage where they thought - let's just go for it!

I think we knew from the outset that our final objective would be Longdon after reaching Teal Inlet and then Estancia House. It was advance to contact because we didn't know if the Argentines had pulled back, we didn't know if Estancia was occupied because SAS had given word that maybe there were 4 men there. I can remember lying in the FUP now, at this tree line - a fir tree, big bushy thing - looking out over towards Estancia, just waiting.

A 'CIVVY' IN 3 PARA
Patrolling Towards Estancia House with D Company
By the late Terry Peck

Touching down at Teal Inlet, I was taken to 3 Para HQ and introduced to Lieutenant Colonel Pike. The HQ had been set up in the settlement store. There were several Officers and NCO's present and most were just finishing a brew. Someone kindly provided me with a 'mixed' meal of 'compo' and I was then introduced to Major Pat Butler, OC D (Patrol) Company. He explained that we would be moving out very soon. During the next few weeks I would get to know Major Butler quite well. He was a man of great courage and stamina, whose first consideration was for the men in his command. I was aware that my presence was the cause of some curiosity among many of the soldiers but there was little time to sit and chat as orders were being given to start their move. I heard a few angry words being expressed about someone who had had a 'negligent

Terry Peck joins D (Patrol Company) of 3 Para for the battle on Longdon, seen here in the background. Terry Peck

discharge' and the guy had been 'casevac'd' with a gunshot wound to his foot.

Teal Inlet was now the front line for 3 Brigade. The settlement was alive with Paras and Royal Marines, together with their Support Companies. Major Butler detailed me to 42 Alpha Patrol, one of the many 4 man teams which constantly carried out reconnaissance ahead of the battalion. Before I could join them a Royal Navy Officer came up to me and wanted to know if the enemy had mined anywhere in Salvador Waters. He had known of my motorbike journey in the preceding weeks and my contacts at Rincon Grande. I explained that to my knowledge the waters were safe. No one in Rincon Grande or Salvador Farm had seen any signs of the enemy operating in the Waters. I had to assume it safe. By now 3 Para had already set off on the gruelling 'tab' to Estancia Farm which would be the next objective. In single file the Battalion were strung out for over a mile. The ground was white with a covering of snow about two inches deep. Each followed in the tracks of the man ahead. Racing along the flanks of the column were a couple of Scorpion tanks giving cover to the advancing troops. Everyone was given a 'ten minute' break every hour or so. Although the pace was slow we were covering the ground very steadily. Fortunately the weather remained kind; an overcast sky and little wind. From time to time, the sound of gunfire could be heard in the distance. I heard from some of the lads that several Argentines had been captured and were being passed down the line.

I had been attempting to make radio contact with Brookfield Farm and Estancia Farm but my batteries had gone flat on me. Obviously they were past their best and were unable to hold a charge for long.

During my second 'break', halfway up the north side of the Mallow Hill, I sat down with a few of the lads and began talking about the recent events. I realised that these were the same chaps whom I had met on my arrival at Port San Carlos a few days ago. I was introduced again to 'Blue' Harding, Pete 'Six Feet' Harden, Joe McKeown, Taff Davis, Dickie Bishop, Raj Rajput and Pete Deakins. I explained that I was a local and had left Stanley several weeks ago, hiding out in the hills. Having learnt that the British Forces had landed, I had made my way to Port San Carlos where I had been invited to join 3 Para. "That's some story", said Blue, "We reckon you're one of the boys who've been having themselves some fun." I laughed and told them that I really was a local, and not part of the Special Forces. Did I really look like an SAS or SBS man? It was several days before they accepted that I really was a local.

It was now late afternoon and we had to make the Mallow Bridge before dark. I was still trying to make radio contact with the Estancia Farm and I would leave the column of troops and make for the high ground in order to get a more direct line of sight to transmit my signal. No doubt the lads thought this strange and probably added weight to their suspicions. Just on dusk we topped the hill and could see the bridge below us. We rested up for an hour at the bridge and everyone set about making a brew. Darkness had fallen and orders were being issued to restart our advance. Everyone formed up in the various units and we set out on the next phase of the march. We knew that the enemy had troops on Mount Vernet, Mount Kent and the Estancia Mountain. I was aware that an enemy patrol would sometimes visit the Estancia Farm. We would be very exposed to the enemy as we advanced across the low ground, as each of the mountains overlooked the land to the west, from where our approach was being made. Through the broken cloud the moon would appear, bathing the ground in a pale light. Everything was going to favour the Argentines. But no, in typical Falklands fashion the weather changed and we found ourselves battling against driving hail and sleet. I had eventually made contact with Trudy Morrison at Brookfield Farm. The transmission was very broken, making it difficult to copy. I gathered that the enemy had visited Estancia Farm the previous day. They were seen to remain for some considerable time in an area east of the farm. She thought they had been sowing 'tatties' (mine laying). This turned out not to be the case.

Progress had slowed, not surprising given the terrible conditions. In the best of weather the terrain we were marching over was some of the worst land in the Falklands. Small steep hills covered in rocks, ' diddle dee' bush and ferns. The deep valleys were mostly flooded or covered in huge bogs. Every man was fully laden, carrying approximately 100 lbs or more. Those carrying the radio equipment far exceeded this weight. I realised that those leading the column were well off course and that if they continued in this direction we would find ourselves cut off by the sea. If one had looked in the direction of Estancia Farm one could have been forgiven for thinking it was a straightforward march but it is deceiving. The land is broken for miles around by tidal waters with many inlets. Long peninsulars stretch towards the sea and there are very few short cuts if the tide is high.

Everyone had gone to ground and apart from a few muffled curses and the occasional 'clink' from someone's kit, all was very quiet. A figure appeared out of the darkness, asking, 'Anyone seen Terry, the civvy? The Boss wants him up front." I clambered to my feet and made myself known. I followed the lad to the front of the column, where I saw several chaps hunched over a map laid out on the ground. "Can you give us some idea where our present position is?" someone asked. In the light of a small torch I pointed out where we were, explaining that we were some 3 miles too far east. We would have to do a sharp right and head west, then turn due south. We would then avoid the inlets and make a crossing at the head of Long Creek. "Would you mind taking over the lead?" This was the first task I had been invited to undertake so I thought I had better get it right. The word was passed back through the troops that there would be a change of direction, which I'm sure wasn't well received.   From memory I visualised our position. We were well down the peninsular and to get back on track we had to move right, making our way along the steep slopes of the peninsular, then swing left towards the distant hills, then left again to bring us near Long Creek. It was a tough detour in the dark, made worse by the steep slippery peat banks, which were 3 - 4 feet high. Slippery rocks and water filled holes added to the problem. At one point I found myself face down in the mud. I had been walking along the top of a peat bank and tumbled over the edge, knocking the wind out of myself. Someone grabbed me by my bergen, and pulled me to my feet and, having managed to get my wind back, we were off again. There must have been many a lad that night who experienced that same horrible feeling of falling down into a black abyss. It may have been only a few feet, but it felt like fifty and with the added weight, the landing was extremely painful.

A few times the word was passed for me to 'slow down'. The sleet and hail had eased off but it was freezing cold. At last I found the vehicle track. Although it was wet and muddy it did make the going easier and I'm sure many were glad to get on to a recognisable route again. The tracked route led towards a creek and making good time we headed down towards the beach. The tide was low so I informed JP (Sergeant John Pettinger) that we could safely cross over the creek, which would cut at least another mile or more off our journey. We finally made base at the head of Double Creek, about two and a half miles south west of Estancia Farm.

The weather had deteriorated very quickly and everyone was totally exhausted but this didn't stop Major Butler issuing orders for our Patrol to carry out a reconnaisance of Estancia Farm. I was to accompany them. Our 8 man patrol was made up of Corporals Dickie Bishop, Joe McKeown, 'Blue' Harding and Pete 'Six Feet' Harden and Privates Pete Deakins, Raj Rajput, 'Taff' Davis, and Dickie Absolon. Leaving the area of Long Creek the patrol spread out in single file with Pete Deakins and myself leading. The wind had dropped but thick snow was still falling. We had covered about half the distance to Estancia Farm when all hell let loose to our front. Bursts of automatic gunfire had opened up ahead. Going to ground we waited until the firing had stopped. Nothing could be seen and the fire had not been directed at our patrol. Using his IWS (individual weapon sight), Pete was unable to pick up any signs of movement so Corporal Bishop gave the order to move on.

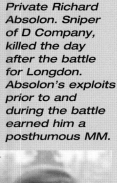

Private Richard Absolon. Sniper of D Company, killed the day after the battle for Longdon. Absolon's exploits prior to and during the battle earned him a posthumous MM.

Being familiar with the layout of the farm, Pete passed his IWS to me. We had now come within a quarter mile of the farm. There had been no further shooting.

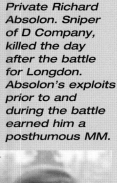

Corporal John Graham and Terry Peck patrol towards Mount Longdon. John Graham.

Lying up on a small ridge I studied the layout of the farm. Apart from a few flurries of snow the worst of the storm seemed to have passed and it was easy to make out the buildings. I could observe no movement - everything looked OK. We had to climb over a couple of wire fences before reaching the first of the outbuildings.

The first, a large Nissen hut used as a shearing shed, was checked out by three lads. They emerged after some minutes, giving it an all clear. The rest of the patrol had taken up an all round defensive role during the search. Next it was on to the smaller sheds and having checked them out we made our way to the main house. Two other store sheds adjacent to the house had to be cleared but these were found locked. The patrol took up various defensive positions around the house, which was in total darkness. There was an eerie silence about the place. Sometimes the moon would break through the cloud, bathing the place in a pale light. Corporal Bishop and I made our way to the house. I indicated that I would knock on a window. The patrol were aware that several civilians had been occupying the house, one a tiny baby. I knocked gently. Silence. I tried a heavier knock. "Who's there? What the fuck do you want?" called a voice I

41

A four man 'recce' patrol from D Company. Left to right: 'Raj' Rajput, Corporal Dickie Bishop, Private Pete Deakins and Corporal Joe McKeown.
Terry Peck.

knew well. "It's me, 'Rubber Duck'. Are there any Argies about?" I answered. "No, but the fucking SAS have been - shot the fuck out of my shed. Hang on, I'll let you in". Moments later the door opened and Tony Heathman appeared, having pulled on trousers and shirt but no footwear. Corporal Bishop, having questioned Tony and satisfied himself that there were no Argentines within the area, called the patrol together and briefed them. Tony had gone back inside and we could hear him talking to other people in the house. The patrol was reorganised to allow each of them an opportunity to have a hot drink and a quick warm up in the house. Going inside I saw Tony's wife, Ailsa, shaking up the Rayburn stove. There was a huge smile on everyone's face, these being the first British troops they had seen. Ailsa, still smiling, pushed a large saucepan onto the hot plate and invited everyone to have some stew. "I bet you're starving. I've got plenty of stew left over from dinner. It'll only take a few minutes to heat up." Typical of Ailsa and Tony, the Guest Book was produced and the lads were invited to sign it! Despite these light moments there was no relaxing and the hot drink and stew were devoured quickly. The rest of the patrol received the same welcome and hospitality. Then it was time to move out. It was colder than ever outside and the ground was beginning to freeze solid. It was agreed that we would lie up for a few hours and make our way back to the battalion to report shortly before dawn.

THE PREPARATIONS

With the British now established on the line of high ground stretching from Mounts Estancia and Vernet in the north through Mount Kent to Mount Challenger in the south, it was essential that Brigadier Thompson and the commanders of 3 Para, 42 and 45 Commandos gathered as much intelligence as possible about the strength and dispositions of the Argentine forces defending Port Stanley in order to inform their planning.

Lieutenant Colonel Pike had already been told that his likely objective would be Mount Longdon, the peak now glowering down on his battalion from the east. Thompson had set the problem and Pike was now left to ponder it. How best to go about cracking this tough nut on the northern flank of the Argentine line which bulged towards 3 Commando Brigade?

Pike established 3 Para just north of the Estancia - Stanley track, some 4km west of the Murrell Bridge which crossed the river of the same name, with A Company forward, B Company just over a mile to the west and C Company on Mount Estancia. A patrol base was established near the track on some low bluffs overlooking the Murrell Bridge. 3 Para observers had already picked up movements on Longdon during the hours of daylight, but long distance observation

Lieutenant Colonel Hew Pike

was not enough. More detailed information about the strength and depth of specific positions, not least about the weaponry available to the Argentines, would have to be gathered. This meant that 3 Para would have to 'go out and find out' and that meant sending out patrols - not only the twelve, four man patrols of D (Patrol) Company under Major Pat Butler but fighting patrols from the rifle companies - to poke and pry amidst the rugged nooks and crannies of Mount Longdon. The problem was the intervening ground. From the Mount Estancia position to Mount

Longdon it is some three miles as the shell flies but there is no high ground in between which could conceal an approach from prying eyes on Longdon. Instead, a wide, featureless valley covered with pale yellow grass opens out and this created a broad No Man's Land between the British and Argentine lines. And so, just as the British had sought to dominate No Man's Land between the opposing lines of trenches on the Western Front during World War One with a philosophy of treating the German wire as the British front line, now Thompson urged his subordinates to dominate the ground, thus retaining the initiative and maintaining momentum. Any 3 Para patrols venturing out onto the bare, bleached backdrop of the valley during daylight would have stood out like a line of black ants on recently laid concrete. Everything would have to be done at night.

Lieutenant Colonel Pike ordered the first probing attack on Mount Longdon to go in on 3rd June but it ran into well-placed Argentine artillery fire and was forced to pull back. It was the first of many. It was difficult for patrols to get out, complete their tasks and get back before first light so patrols went out and stayed out for two and sometimes three nights, lying up during daylight hours and completing their tasks in darkness. Using the forward patrol base as a staging post meant that the distance the patrols had to travel from the Estancia position was reduced but such a position so close to Longdon also drew unwanted attention as Argentine units were also out and about in No Man's Land gathering intelligence. In fact there were so many units - both British and Argentine army and special forces units - squeezed into a comparatively small area that Major David Collett commanding A Company complained that there were '...too many guys out front wandering around recce-ing ... strategic troops operating alongside tactical troops which is not the best way of doing it.' [1] After a sharp firefight with Argentine Special Forces of Compania de Commando 601 and Compania de Fuerzas Especiales 601 de Gendarmerie Nacional, the patrol base was withdrawn on 4th June. Nevertheless the patrols had done some excellent work - work which Brigadier Thompson recognised as being of a 'very high standard indeed' - and had penetrated deep into the Argentine positions.[2] Patrols still went out, albeit over a much greater distance now, and little by little over the following six days the pieces of the Argentine defensive jigsaw on Longdon began to fall into place and a picture began to emerge. This was translated into a scale model of Longdon that became festooned with white tape, white markers and twigs representing Argentine minefields, bunkers and machine gun positions respectively, as more and more information was gathered.

Brigadier Thompson's blueprint for the investment of Stanley had begun to take shape from 6th June. Resisting pressure for a 'narrow front' attack along the Fitzroy-Stanley track, which the Argentine commander Menéndez had expected until as late as 24th May, Brigadier Thompson developed a three-phase operation, each phase peeling away the three successive layers of Argentine defences until Stanley itself was revealed. The first, and perhaps with hindsight, the most crucial phase, was the 3 Commando Brigade assault on the outer defence zone - the outer ring marked by the peaks of Mount Longdon to the north through Two Sisters and down to Mount Harriet in the south.

It was important to seize and secure all three first phase objectives but the capture of Mount Longdon was vital to the success of Brigadier Thompson's overall scheme in that artillery, ammunition and all supplies required to support the entire operation would have to pass north of Mount Kent on their way from the forward logistics base at Teal Inlet. Equally important was securing the route for heliborne traffic in the opposite direction.

'The significance of Longdon was its key position dominating the supply route to Teal Inlet. It was proved vital during the battle, and at times on the following days and nights when the low cloud on the high ground prevented helicopter casevac to Fitzroy. My Brigade Forward Dressing Station at Teal was the only FDS able to accept casualties - for example the Scots Guards casualties were dealt with at Teal and not by their own Brigade FDS at Fitzroy. Incidentally the Divisional Medical Officer wanted to close Teal, but I objected and Jeremy Moore [Major General Jeremy Moore, Divisional Commander and Brigadier Thompson's immediate superior] supported my objection.' [3]

Lieutenant Colonel Pike was briefed on the plan on 10th June. The assault would be a night attack and was to be 'silent to contact' - that is without the support of a preliminary bombardment to 'soften up' the Argentine positions. Brigadier Thompson's reasoning for this was twofold:

'I was keen for all attacks on night 11th /12th June to be silent in order to:

a. preserve surprise as to our objectives and axes.

b. preserve ammunition, bearing in mind the problems with bringing it forward. In the end, after the night's battle, the ammunition on the gun lines was down to a handful per gun on some battery positions. It was this that made any exploitation on to Tumbledown in daylight unwise, so I stopped 45 Commando from advancing from Two Sisters. It became even more important to have the Longdon and Two Sisters assaults silent once I had allowed the attack on Harriet to be 'noisy', as part of the CO of 42 Commando's deception plan, as I hoped the 'noise' in the south would convince the enemy that our axis was along the Fitzroy-Stanley track from the southwest (which he expected), and conceal our approach from the northwest.' [4]

In addition, the experiences of 2 Para at Goose Green had proved how a battle during daylight across open slopes could become stalled and ultimately costly in terms of casualties. Brigadier Thompson's faith in the abilities of his Brigade to carry out a night assault was unshakeable. The possibility of confusion during a night attack on Mount Longdon, a very complex operation fraught with difficulties, would be more than offset by the skill, the discipline, the motivation and leadership of 3 Para.

Lieutenant Colonel Pike now passed down Brigade orders through his own battalion chain of command; first to his company commanders, who would brief their platoon commanders, who in turn would inform their section commanders and the rest of the men, until everyone was aware of their role in the coming battle.

'WORK HARD.'

Longdon Preparations
By Nick Rose ex 6 Platoon, B Company 3 Para.

We'd seen Longdon before because we'd been up and done recce' patrols. We'd been in and out for the week before - a lot of patrolling done. They were having a good old look. They did very well. SAS were definitely playing up there and by that time it had all been plotted, mortar planned, DF'd [defensive fire - pre-registered fire from a variety of weapons - usually by defensive troops] and NGFS [Naval Gun Fire Support]

The general plan was given to us. 'This is what we need to do and your part will be....'

I remember seeing models and getting the 'execution, general outline'. You're given the complete briefing as per orders along the lines of , 'patrol platoon have found a position here that we believe to be a 50mil machine gun and there's going to be another one of those in defilade or enfilade or whatever because a forward recce patrol from A Company bumped into one' etc. etc. So there's all the intelligence side but I can recall the thing that was drilled into us was the fact that you just had to keep going because if you don't the whole thing just breaks down. You just cannot have a clinical sort of approach on a feature like Longdon. You know exactly what it looks like but when you go past features there could be hidden trenches and you might not see them and remember its night time as well. There could be threats coming from any area so you're advancing all the time.

We had a few company briefings about the current situation - what the greater plan was - and then it obviously broke down into platoon briefings with Jon Shaw, [6 Platoon CO]. A good man. He was very thorough about what we needed to do. It was quite a stirring thing. I remember his final point. It was simple - 'work hard'.

Sixty-six years on from the preliminaries prior to the Battle of the Somme in the rear areas of Picardy, the scenes were repeated as British soldiers once more gathered around scale models of their objectives to discuss opposition strong points, terrain and tactics but this time they were 8000 miles away from the battlefields of northern France. When his turn came, Major Peter Dennison, the widely respected commanding officer of the 3 Para Support Company, strode up to the fifty strong sustained fire role machine gunners, mortar men and Milan anti-tank teams clustered around the model of Mount Longdon and commenced his briefing. 'Gents' he said, 'this is it.' [5]

THE PLAN

Lieutenant Colonel Pike's plan for the Longdon attack was based on the sum of his knowledge gained by the British patrols regarding the strength and depth of the Argentine positions and the overall scheme involving 3 Commando Brigade. Intelligence was, by necessity incomplete as the Argentine defenders had been on Longdon since 18th April and so had had almost two months in which to establish themselves on its craggy fastness. Inevitably there would be positions that had not been logged.

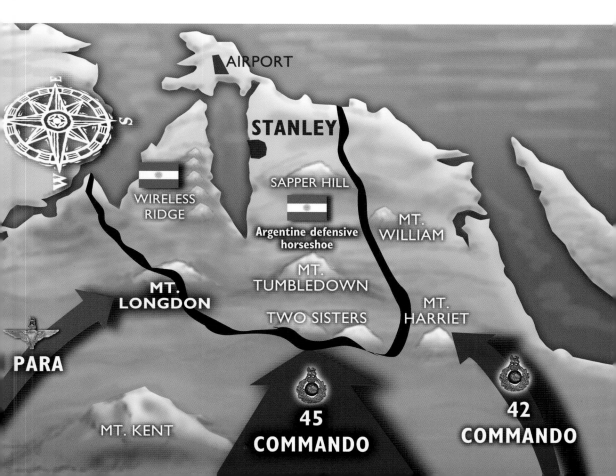

It was already a given that his attack would go in during the hours of darkness and that the advance to contact would be 'silent' but Pike had other considerations as he mulled over his options for an operation the like of which had not been 'undertaken by the battalion for a generation'[1]. Longdon, at only 612ft at its highest point, was not a great height in itself but it dominated the surrounding low lying and open ground for 1km in all directions, whilst known minefields to the south and the presence of Argentine forces on Wireless Ridge to the east effectively ruled out any possibility of a flanking attack. The shape and orientation of Longdon - a narrow, west-east feature consisting of two unequal summits with a saddle like depression separating them - dictated that no more than a force amounting to a single company could operate along its spine at any one time. Pike thus determined to assault the mountain frontally from its western extremity with two of his three rifle companies 'up'.

Using nicknames plucked from the sports fields on which the Rugby Union code is played, to denote key features on the field of battle, A and B Companies would move up from the Estancia position in darkness and cross the 'start line' (codename 'Free Kick') - a fast flowing stream 1km west of Longdon, twisting north towards the Furze Bush Pass and at right angles to the intended line of advance - at 8.01 local time. A Company, (Major David Collett), was to advance on the left, northerly flank, to attack and secure a spur to the northeast (codename 'Wing Forward') and establish a fire base from which it could support B Company, (Major Mike Argue), fighting its way up to and through the forward, western summit of the main feature (codename 'Fly Half') and on to tackle the rear, eastern summit (codename 'Full Back').

The remaining rifle company, C Company (Major Martin Osborne), was to remain on the line of 'Free Kick' as battalion reserve with orders to reinforce the forward platoons should Argentine resistance crumble and the possibility of further exploitation onto Wireless Ridge present itself. This flexibility was built into the overall plan but it was also dependent on 45 Commando taking all its first phase objectives and pushing onto and occupying Tumbledown to the southeast. Also on the start line were the sustained fire role GPMG – 30,000 rounds – and Milan anti-tank teams of Support Company (Major Peter Dennison) who were also to hold on 'Free Kick' ready to go forward when the call came. The Mortar Platoon (Captain Julian James) had also established a mortar line nearby. In charge of casevac and ammunition resupply by means of Volvo BV tracked vehicles was battalion second in command Major Roger Patton supported by Captain Bob Darby.

Ready, and on priority call to provide additional, 'heavier' direct support, Lieutenant Colonel Pike could draw on the services of the six, 105mm light field guns of 79 (Kirkee) Battery, 29 Commando Regiment Royal Artillery and dedicated Naval Gun Fire Support from HMS *Avenger*'s formidable 4.5inch gun, guided in by specialist Naval Gun Fire Observer, Captain Willie McCracken of 148 Battery R.A.

Major Argue's B Company, which would first have to ascend Longdon's western wall and then engage known key points of resistance along the entire length of its craggy spine, faced a daunting task. Although Pike's appreciation of the narrow nature of the Longdon summit had led him to the conclusion that only one company could fight on it at any one time, there was still the possibility that that company

4 Platoon, 3 Para on board the Canberra. *Lieutenant Andrew Bickerdike (middle row, fourth left), with Sergeant Ian McKay to his left. Ian McKay and Privates Neil Grose (top row, third left), Jason Burt (top row, fifth right) and Ian Scrivens (front row, left) will all lose thier lives.* Andrew Bickerdike

might not have sufficient numbers to comb out all the Argentine sangars if some men were held in reserve. To counter this possible scenario, Major Argue hit upon a bold and, some would say, rather risky, model. He decided to advance all his three platoons simultaneously and use them to roll like a tidal wave, up towards 'Fly Half' to break its resistance before sweeping on along the crest of Longdon, swamping the remaining Argentine positions as they went. Running from north to south 4 Platoon (Lieutenant Andrew Bickerdike) was handed the responsibility of clearing the northern face, 5 Platoon (Lieutenant Mark Cox) was to drive up higher then fight along the spine in the centre, whilst 6 Platoon (Lieutenant Jon Shaw) would sweep up from the southwest and seize the southern slopes.

It should be noted that the various plans, developed both at battalion and company level, were not without their detractors. There were some - officers and senior NCOs amongst them - who felt that it was worth dispensing with the element of surprise offered by a silent night attack, in order to have secured the possible benefits of a preliminary bombardment. Longdon had, they reasoned, been subject to harassing fire from 29 Commando Regiment since 3rd June. Further shelling may not have given the game away when the time came to attack. Later the thought, doubtless strengthened by Brigadier Thompson's own admission in his memoir of the war, that the repeated success of D Company patrols in penetrating the Argentine defences and returning unscathed had somehow lulled Lieutenant Colonel Pike and Brigadier Thompson into the mistaken belief that Longdon could be disposed of quickly, perhaps without any prior 'softening up', gained ground.[2] Strategically, however,

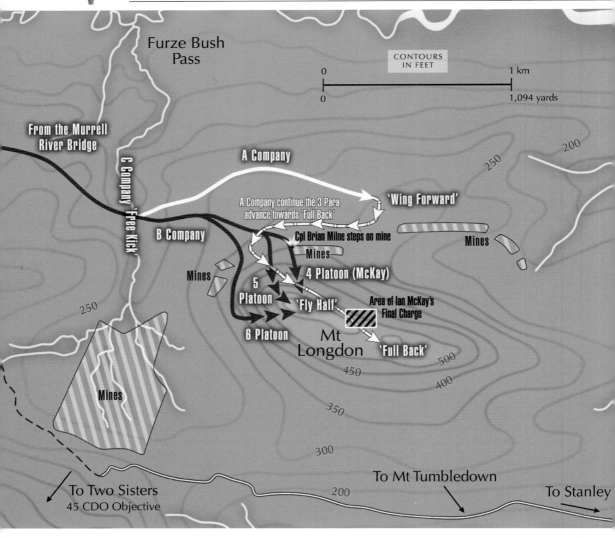

Furze Bush Pass

CONTOURS IN FEET

0   1 km

0   1,094 yards

From the Murrell River Bridge

C Company 'Free Kick'

A Company

A Company continue the 3 Para advance towards 'Full Back'

'Wing Forward'

Cpl Brian Milne steps on mine

Mines

Mines

B Company

Mines

Mines

4 Platoon (McKay)

5 Platoon

'Fly Half'

Area of Ian McKay's Final Charge

6 Platoon

Mt Longdon

'Full Back'

Mines

250

250

200

500

450

400

350

300

200

To Two Sisters
45 CDO Objective

To Mt Tumbledown

To Stanley

THE PLAN - BATTLE FOR MOUNT LONGDON

there could have been serious consequences if HQ 3 Commando Brigade had been too prodigal of artillery ammunition during the initial phase of the final battles for Stanley. With Longdon still defiant, the supply line to Teal was not yet secure and even without a preliminary bombardment, ammunition on the gun lines was later found to have dipped to just a handful of rounds per battery in some cases at the end of the first night's fighting. Brigadier Thompson felt he had to concentrate on the broader picture and conserve artillery stocks for the latter phases as well as deceiving the Argentines into believing his main thrust would come from the south with a 'noisy' operation on Mount Harriet.

THE
ARGENTINES

nitial British estimates of the strength of the Argentine forces on Mount Longdon proved over generous. At one stage during the probing phase between 1st June and the eve of battle on 11th June, a figure of 800 Argentines in the area of Mount Longdon and Wireless Ridge was being suggested. In fact, by the time 3 Para were ready to attack there was only one company of infantry - reinforced by two 'grupos' of Marine Infantry machine gunners and riflemen (24 men in total) with six, Browning 12.7mm heavy machine guns - and a reserve platoon of engineers in position on the mountain.

ARGENTINE FORCES ON MOUNT LONGDON 11TH /12TH JUNE 1982

R.I. 7
Regimiento de Infanteria Mecanizado 7 (7th Mechanised Infantry Regiment)

Based - La Tablada, Buenos Aires Province

CO - Lieutenant Colonel Omar Gimenez
2 i/c - Major Carlos Carrizo - Salvadores
Arrived Falkland Islands 14th April 1982
Deployed 17th April to Sector Plata (Silver) - Mount Longdon, Wireless Ridge, Moody Brook. HQ Moody Brook.
Carrizo-Salvadores given command of Sector Silver 2 (Longdon) on 17th April

TOTAL FORCE OF 287 MEN

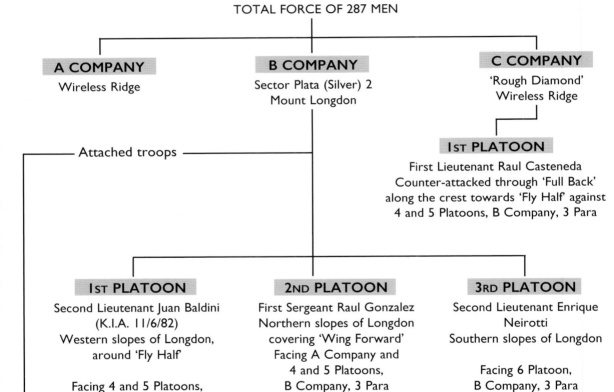

A COMPANY
Wireless Ridge

B COMPANY
Sector Plata (Silver) 2
Mount Longdon

C COMPANY
'Rough Diamond'
Wireless Ridge

1st PLATOON
First Lieutenant Raul Casteneda
Counter-attacked through 'Full Back'
along the crest towards 'Fly Half' against
4 and 5 Platoons, B Company, 3 Para

— Attached troops —

1st PLATOON
Second Lieutenant Juan Baldini
(K.I.A. 11/6/82)
Western slopes of Longdon,
around 'Fly Half'

Facing 4 and 5 Platoons,
B Company, 3 Para

2nd PLATOON
First Sergeant Raul Gonzalez
Northern slopes of Longdon
covering 'Wing Forward'
Facing A Company and
4 and 5 Platoons,
B Company, 3 Para

3rd PLATOON
Second Lieutenant Enrique
Neirotti
Southern slopes of Longdon

Facing 6 Platoon,
B Company, 3 Para

**1st Platoon Compania de Ingenieros X
(X Brigade Engineers)**

Lieutenant Hugo Quiroga
Reserve - in and around 'Full Back'
Moved forward to support the line east of 'Fly Half'
against 4, 5 and 6 Platoons,
B Company, 3 Para

**2x Grupos (¹/₃ section) Compania de
Ametrallodoras 12.7 Infanteria Marina
(Marine Infantry 12.7 Machine Gun
Company)**

24 men - 6x Browning 12.7m.m. (0.50 heavy
machine guns) with supporting rifles
Dispersed among defending platoons

The men belonged to B Company of the 7th Regimiento de Infanteria de Mecanizado - 7th Mechanized Infantry Regiment (R.I.7) - of X Mechanized Infantry Brigade, which had arrived in the Falklands on 14th April. R.I.7 had been deployed to Sector Plata (Silver) Including Mount Longdon, Wireless Ridge and Moody Brook and became part of a force of 8,500 - 9,000 men of 6 infantry units which eventually faced the seven British infantry units which converged on Stanley.

R.I.7 was based at La Tablada in the province of Buenos Aires and was made up of some 700 recalled reservists and men in their second year of their two years' compulsory service. They were certainly not 'raw' recruits, although some, like Anglo-Argentine 'colimba' - conscript - Michael Savage, would admit to being vastly ill-prepared to meet the likes of the men of 3 Para on a bitter winter's night on an inhospitable mountain top on East Falkland. The only 'military training he had received had occurred 16 months before and had consisted mainly of marching, saluting and cleaning toilets. He had spent just two days training with a rifle and had 'served' at a desk' in an office for a year. Michael at least felt like a 'civilian' when he took his position with C Company R.I.7 on a feature called 'Rough Diamond' just north east of Longdon towards Wireless Ridge.

Savage's grandmother had been born to British parents who had migrated to Argentina in the nineteenth century and the family remained deeply proud of its British heritage. Such had been the pull that his grandfather, although Argentine by birth, had served with the R.A.F. during World War Two. Michael spoke fluent English and British traditions and customs were observed in the Savage household. He had played cricket with British friends at boarding school in Buenos Aires. There were others with the same background and with English surnames. He shared a trench with a friend called Alan Craig. These men would soon have to fight others who 'were as good as family'.

The defence of Longdon was entrusted to R.I.7 Second-in-Command, Major Carlos Carrizo-Salvadores who first set foot on Longdon on 17th April. The next day the three platoons of B Company set to work on building their defences in anticipation of an attack from the north. They had the best part of the next eight weeks to dig into the peat banks, hew positions out of the unforgiving rock, cover bunkers with corrugated iron and put stone slabs and peat turves on top, making sure that all approaches up the mountain towards the western and eastern summits were covered with interlocking arcs of fire. Major Carrizo-Salvadores would switch his positions after 24th May so that they faced west, with a concentration of sangars among and around the western summit 'Fly Half'. There they waited.

These men would soon have to fight others who 'were as good as family'.

The grandfather of Michael Savage wearing his RAF uniform during World War Two. Michael Savage

'Colimbas'. Michael Savage (first on left) and fellow conscripts pose for the camera near their base in Argentina prior to the war. Michael Savage

Many, including Michael Savage, consider themselves the 'forgotten army'

There has been much debate surrounding the fate of these men in the mountains of the outer defence zone. Many, including Michael Savage, consider themselves the 'forgotten army', abandoned by their officers and left to survive on a diet of thin, lukewarm soup, pasta and *maté*, a bitter herbal tea. Some took to walking miles and risking heavy penalties to steal from the supply dumps near Stanley, while others shot and roasted sheep on old bedframes. There are others who maintain that these men were helped to make themselves as comfortable as possible under the circumstances and that their officers tried hard to bolster morale. Michael Savage's weight dipped to 55 kilos after two months on Longdon and nothing had prepared him for the terrain he found there. As the weather deteriorated he became more and more 'terrified'. Nevertheless, when the time came, the Argentine soldiers would stand and fight.

THE WEAPONS

3 **Para embarked on the Falklands campaign with an array of weaponry which combined to produce a formidable level of firepower. The most ubiquitous weapon was the standard issue rifle carried by British infantrymen at the time - the 7.62mm calibre L1A1S.L.R. or self loading rifle. This rifle was a British adaptation of an original Belgian F.N., F.A.L.(fusil automatique leger) design. The British variant, arrived at after an extensive series of field trials and modifications, eliminated the automatic fire feature of the original design and thus only fired single shots, the theory being that this encouraged men to consider their targets and fire with greater accuracy, rather than wasting ammunition in general and sustained bursts. Nonetheless, during the fighting on Longdon, such had been the training with this reliable and well manufactured weapon, that the paras were able to lay down a considerable level of co-ordinated fire on suspected Argentine positions.**

The L1A1 bayonet, which was designed to be fitted to the S.L.R., had a blade of 204mm (8 inches) and, due to the nature of the close quarters fighting, in and around Argentine bunkers, became an invaluable weapon in its own right.

Another weapon which was widespread throughout the battalion was the fully automatic, 7.62mm calibre G.P.M.G., the General Purpose Machine Gun, universally known as the 'Gimpy'. Again this was based on a Belgian F.N. design and was employed both as a section fire support weapon-one per section-and in a sustained fire (S.F.) role. In the section support role the Gimpy was mounted on a lightweight bipod but when grouped together in the Machine Gun platoon it was fitted with an S.F. kit consisting of a heavy tripod, at least three heavier barrels - two of these were spares in case of overheating - and a dial sight which enabled it to fire sustained bursts on pre-registered targets otherwise obscured from view. The weapon was used in this role in Major Dennison's Support Company and several teams pushed up into advanced positions near 'Fly Half' on Longdon to provide fire support for the beleaguered rifle companies

For those men such as radio operators or senior Non Commissioned Officers whose tasks or duties made it difficult for them to carry an S.L.R., the option was the 9mm calibre L2A3 Sterling submachine gun. This compact - the stock could be folded to reduce stowage space - and fully automatic weapon, fired pistol ammunition from a curved 34 round magazine inserted on the left. R.S.M Lawrie Ashbridge was famously photographed in Port San Carlos carrying a Sterling S.M.G.

Also providing much needed support for the rifle companies during the battle was the 'state of the art' Euromissile MILAN wire-guided, anti-tank weapon system just entering service with the British Army in 1982. The MILANS, consisting of a control/firing post and missile in a launch tube, were grouped together in the anti-tank platoon under Captain Tony Mason, along with the WOMBAT 120mm recoilless anti-tank guns. The WOMBAT was not used on Longdon but the MILAN teams were ordered up on to the western slopes where the high explosive missiles were brought into action to engage Argentine sangars in a 'bunker busting' role. The MILAN teams obviously became prime targets for the Argentine defenders and three men from one MILAN team Privates Hedicker, West and McCarthy, were amongst the last fatalities of the battalion.

The mortar deployed in the Mortar Platoon of Support Company under the command of Captain Julian James, was the standard issue British 81mm infantry weapon in an indirect fire role. The range of the 81mm, when firing high explosive shells, was more than 5000 metres and a well trained team could expect to put at least twelve rounds a minute onto the target.

Those men designated as specialist snipers were armed with the 7.62mm calibre L42A1 rifle, a weapon used only in this role. The L42A1 used the basic Lee Enfield manual bolt mechanism which had changed little since the 1890s and was a conversion of the World War Two .303 calibre rifle. The important conversions concerned a new barrel and new magazine adapted to take 7.62mm ammunition, along with changes to the trigger mechanisms and fixed sights. The old World War Two Mark 3 telescopic sight and mounting was retained. This weapon was used by Private Richard Absolon of D (Patrol) Company during his extensive patrolling, sniping and escort duties prior to and during the battle. Absolon was killed on the morning after Longdon had been taken but his exemplary service was recognised with the award of a posthumous Military Medal.

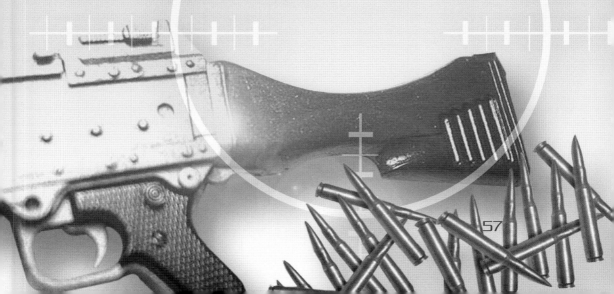

① 7.62MM GENERAL PURPOSE MACHINE GUN

② BRITISH L1A1 - SLR

③ SNIPER RIFLE L42A1

④ L2A3 STERLING SUB-MACHINE GUN

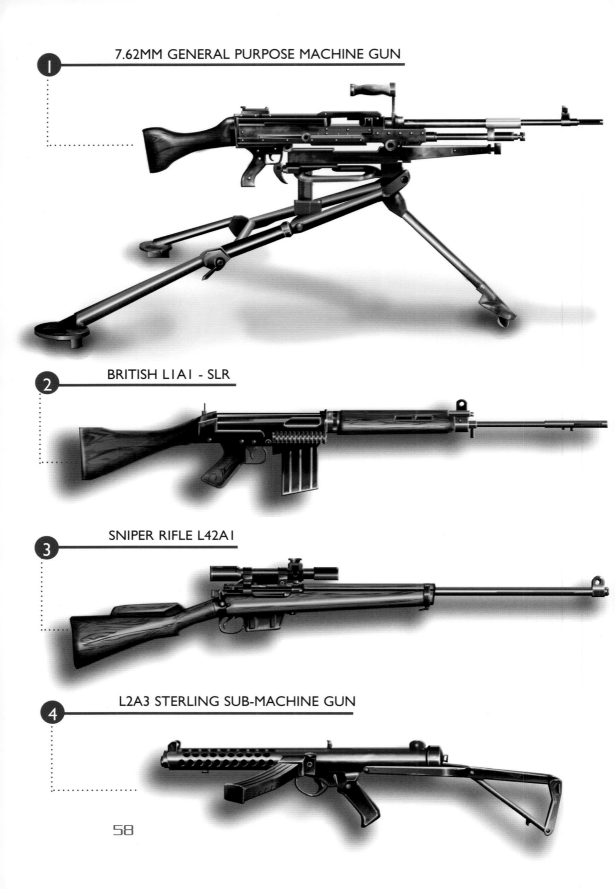

58

MILAN ANTI-TANK GUIDED WEAPON **5**

L1A1 - SLR BAYONET **6**

L16A2 81MM MORTAR **7**

BROWNING FN HIGH POWER PISTOL **8**

Illustrations by Jon Wilkinson.

TECHNICAL SPECIFICATIONS

1 **7.62MM GENERAL PURPOSE MACHINE GUN**

Calibre: 7.62mm • **Weight:** 13.85kg (gun plus 50 round belt)
Length: 1230mm (light role) • **Barrel length:** 629mm
Muzzle velocity: 838m/s • **Feed:** 100-round disintegrating-link belt
Effective range: 800m light role, 1800m sustained fire role (tracer burn out at 1100m)Cyclic rate of fire 750 rounds per minute

2 **BRITISH L1A1 - SLR**

Calibre: 7.62mm • **Weight:** 5kg loaded
Length: 1143mm • **Barrel length:** 554mm
Muzzle velocity: 838m (2,750ft) per second • **Magazine:** 20 round box
Effective range: 30-40 rpm (single shot)

3 **SNIPER RIFLE L42A1**

Calibre: 7.62mm • **Weight:** 4.43 kg loaded
Length: 1181mm • **Barrel length:** 699mm
Muzzle velocity: 838m (2,750ft) per second • **Magazine:** 10 rounds

4 **L2A3 STERLING SUB-MACHINE GUN**

Calibre: 9mm • **Weight:** 3.47 kg loaded
Length: 690mm extended stock - 483mm folded • **Barrel length:** 198mm
Muzzle velocity: 390m (2,750ft) per second • **Magazine:** 10 or 34 round
Cyclic rate of fire: 550 rpm

5 **MILAN ANTI-TANK GUIDED WEAPON**

Dimensions: length 0.769m, diameter 9cm, span 26.5cm
Launch weight: missile 6.65kg, complete unit 16.5kg
Propulsion: Solid-propellant booster/sustainer rocket
Performance: range 2,000 m • **Warhead:** 2.98 kg hollow charge HE
Armour penetration: 650mm (25.6 in)

6 **L1A1 - SLR BAYONET**

Blade length: 204mm (8 inches)

7 **L16A2 81MM MORTAR**

Calibre: 81mm • **Weight:** 37.94 kg • **Barrel length:** 1280mm
Muzzle velocity: 225m/s • **Magazine range HE:** 5,650m • **Rate of Fire:** 15 rpm

8 **BROWNING FN HIGH POWER PISTOL**

Calibre: 9mm • **Weight:** 1.04 kg loaded
Length: 200mm • **Barrel length:** 118mm
Muzzle velocity: 350m (1,148ft) per second • **Magazine:** 14 rounds

THE BATTLE

Ith June 1982 - a little before 8.15 pm local time. Back home in Britain it was almost the height of summer but on East Falkland down in the South Atlantic it was the middle of winter. Now, pausing at a line of white mine marker tape laid by D Company on the eastern banks of a small stream flowing north towards the Murrell River at Furze Bush Pass, the assaulting platoons of A and B Companies gathered their thoughts as NCOs moved up and down the lines giving their final words of encouragement. This was their 'start line' - codename 'Free Kick'. It was dark, it was bitterly cold and icy water had penetrated the boots and socks of some who had fallen thigh deep in the stream they had just forded. The sweat - the combined result of anxiety and extreme exertion - which had lathered their bodies on the tab across country from the Estancia position, was now doing its work; lowering body temperatures as the biting wind penetrated trusty, loaned SAS windproofs.

Guided in by Falkland Islander Vernon Steen, they were late, but not by much. It was to 3 Para's credit that, as the seconds ticked by, they were coming up to being just fourteen minutes behind schedule. The approach had been difficult. Each man carried a personal load in the region of 100 lbs, a colossal weight to carry into an attack, that consisted of their personal stocks of food and water, rifle, bayonet, spare magazines stuffed into every pouch of webbing and smock pockets, 400-600 rounds of linked ammunition for the GPMGs and several fragmentation or phosphorous grenades. Some men carried three plastic 66mm LAWs and a couple of 84s for the Carl Gustav Rocket Launchers. Others in Support Company carried tripods for the sustained fire role GPMGs and Milan missiles strapped below radios on their backs. They had already marched for more than three hours, held up by delays in crossing the Murrell River and confusion resulting from Support Company 'cutting up' and separating the advancing platoons of B Company. They still had some way to go to reach the lowers slopes of their objective.

It would soon be time. High up in his command post towards the rear summit - 'Full Back' - of the Argentine defences on Longdon, Major Carizzo-Salvadores and some of his HQ staff tuned in their small receiver to hear the voice of Pope John Paul II, who had arrived in Argentina that day, celebrating Mass at the National Shrine at Lujan. As the blessing began Salvadores' three platoon commanders called in. They had nothing to report. 1,500 metres away down the slopes of the mountain to the west CSM John Weeks was also pointing his men in the direction of The Almighty only his delivery was rather more prosaic than that of the Pontiff. 'If any of you fuckin' want to pray then here's your chance to really fucking talk to the man upstairs because you'll need him throughout the night.' [1] Section commanders were also doing their best to invoke divine intervention. Corporal Trevor Wilson's brief to Private Nick Rose and the rest of 3 Section was short and to the point; 'say your prayers lads.'

'The sound of 120 plus bayonets clicking into place seemed to carry for miles on the swirling wind.'

Major Carrizo-Salvadores had already ordered the Rasit ground surveillance radar, sited on Longdon's western slopes with Lieutenant Baldini's forward 1st platoon, to be switched off, fearing that its signal would be picked up by the British. The decision was to help Shaw's B Company during the initial stages of its advance. Nevertheless between 'Free Kick' and Longdon there was still a minefield to negotiate.

When the order came to 'fix bayonets' the men of B Company finally realised that they had reached the point of no return. In the deafening silence before battle, the barely audible sound of 120 plus bayonets clicking into place seemed to carry for miles on the swirling wind.[2] Would the Argentines hear? This was it.

At 8.15 p.m., more than 200 men of A and B Companies stepped over the white tape and into the unknown. A Company headed for First Sergeant Gonzales's 2nd Platoon defending the north western slopes and 'Wing Forward', whilst 4, 5 and 6 platoons of B Company advanced at a steady pace and shook out into assault formation as the rising moon began to illuminate the crags and the narrow, steep sided rock runs which seamed the lower slopes. Further up, the splintered outcrops of rock that marked the western summit of Fortress Longdon loomed above them. There was 'Fly Half'. There was their destination.

On the right flank of B Company, the men of 6 Platoon made for the southern approaches to 'Fly Half', guided by Corporal Jerry Phillips of D Company, veteran of several Longdon patrols, and after about an hour, hit the forward slopes and began their ascent. They had crossed the 1000 metres of intervening ground in silence save for the rhythmic 'swish, swish' of their DMS boots brushing against the tussock grass. Private Nick Rose checked his position in his four-man team and followed his section commander, Corporal Trevor Wilson, -'... perfect as a section commander. He was a real soldier's soldier and knew the score' - up the hill. The overpowering smell of human faeces invaded Rose's nostrils as he went on - a hint of slack Argentine organisation in the field? 'They *did not know* we were there.' Still silence. Were they really going to pull this off?

Suddenly and violently, Nick Rose heard the silence ripped apart somewhere off to his left as the left forward section commander of 4 Platoon, Corporal Brian

Milne, stepped on a mine and screamed out in agony. The mountain exploded into life as the Argentine forward bunkers and Rasit section under Sergeant Nista of Baldini's 1st Platoon came into action, spraying 4 and 5 Platoons on the northwestern slopes with fire interspersed with green tracer rounds. Argentine mortar and artillery batteries were called up and rounds were soon thumping the ground behind the paras. The battle for Longdon had been joined. Ahead lay ten hours of the most unimaginable and bloody, hand-to-hand gutter fighting.

In spite of the Argentine fire, 6 Platoon under Lieutenant Jon Shaw continued its climb up the southern flanks towards 'Fly Half' virtually unopposed. Private Nick Rose glanced left and saw the flashes of British red and Argentine green tracer dancing up and down the hillside. He remembers thinking it looked just like a two-way firing range. He knew they were now moving through Argentine positions; he could see their sangars for himself.

> **'They don't know we are here, we can still get up there and do the job.'**

'When we went up we weren't really sussed until we'd got at least half-way up the side of Longdon. Jerry Phillips took us up there and he ended

MOUNT LONGDON - BATTLE ON THE WESTERN SLOPES 11th - 12th JUNE 1982

FLY HALF

O WING
ORWARD

FULL
BACK

2nd PLATOON
7 IR

1st PLATOON
7 IR

6 PLATOON
B COMPANY
3 PARA

ATOON
MPANY
PARA

3 PARA
REGIMENTAL
AID POST (RAP)

3rd PLATOON
7 IR

PLATOON
COMPANY
3 PARA

A COMPANY
3 PARA

up shot in the arm. 'Meccano Man' we used to call him - he had his arm pounded. Every bone was broken and he had sort of 'meccano' built into it and it grew again. We're still going up and Jerry says, "They don't know we are here, we can still get up there and do the job." So we did. There was myself, the Platoon Sergeant Pete Grey, Tony Greenwood and 'Baz' Barratt who advanced as a four-man, half section on the left hand side as we approached and breasted the top, going through a fire position. We went into sort of extended line and took cover and, 'bang, bang, bang,' just unloaded. We just 'laced' the place - laid it down thick and heavy, hard and fast and started moving forward into whatever cover we could get. It was massive, rapid fire - suppressive fire - into our general area of our responsibility. We just flooded the place, 'stonked' it. When the dust started to clear we looked for likely enemy positions and then put some rounds into those. It was 'recce' by fire' but we were doing it intelligently.

Then the training kicks in. It does take over. You know where you should go. You think, "If I go there, 'bang' I'm going to get done, because it's just such a likely place for a GPMG to be covering". So we work on movement with covering fire. We're shouting to each other now, "O.K. we're going left." And so you move forward. You move where you think it's the right place to go and it is - most of the time. Sometimes it doesn't work. But then it started to break down because there were snipers with night sights, which was extremely damaging.'

> **' I could hear my men being killed. They had only just woken up and now they were dying.'**

The men were into and through Corporal Oscar Carrizo's section of Lieutenant Neirotti's 3rd Platoon before some of the Argentines had had time to rouse themselves from their slumbers. It was a vulnerable time for the Argentines as new sentries had just been posted.

'I'd got three men around me - remembered Rose, - Pete Grey, 'Baz' Barratt and Tony Greenwood - and there's another eight guys in the middle section of our area and then another six to eight guys on the far right hand side - among them were Den Dunn, Trev Wilson, a bloke called Shaw, he was a craftsman [R.E.M.E. attached 3 Para], 'Taff' Power, and Stu Gray.'

Corporal Carrizo recalled how his section was quickly engulfed by Rose and his comrades,

'Outside the English were running past, screaming to each other and firing into tents and bunkers. I could hear my men being killed. They had only just woken up and now they were dying. I could hear muffled explosions followed by cries, helpless cries. I knew grenades were being thrown into the bunkers in the follow-up. The Sergeant and I discussed surrendering, but decided we'd wait until it was over. All we could do was wait. The English were all around us. They had arrived within seconds, like lightning. I prayed and prayed a grenade wouldn't come into our bunker. The sheer mental pressure exhausted me.' [3]

Now, galvanised by the will to survive, the Argentine defence in 6 Platoon's area bristled into life. Sections under Corporals Diaz and Pedemonte, backed up by the fire from one of the six, heavy Browning 12.7mm machine gun of the Marine Infantry under Corporal Lamas on the right of Neirotti's position, joined in sweeping the western and southwestern slopes with fire. Lieutenant Neirotti was wounded so Captain Lopez took over to organise the defence as the first of the British shells called in by Captain Willie McCracken began to fall towards 'Full Back'.

Over on the other side of Longdon but further down the slope, Lieutenant Mark Cox's 5 Platoon had been fighting hard for almost an hour. Almost into the Argentine positions by the time Corporal Milne had stepped on the mine, 5 Platoon had borne the brunt of the first Argentine fusillade and had made it to the rockline. The route to the summit here was channelled with the steep sided, west-east orientated rock runs and jagged outcrops that served to funnel the paras into pre-registered killing zones. Now 5 Platoon faced a long and painful struggle if they were to haul themselves to the summit. As their training too 'kicked in', so they broke down into smaller 'fire and movement units'; groups working forward independently, some men drenching sangars with rifle, 66mm LAW or 84mm rocket fire before others rushed forward to take it with bomb and bayonet. Then there would be a pause whilst another objective was identified only for the entire process to be repeated a little further up the hill. It was painstaking and hazardous work made all the more deadly as the Argentines tossed grenades down the stone runs up which the paras were obliged to advance, raining searing fragments of metal and lethal stone chips down on them. Metre by metre 5 platoon clawed its way upward and finally silenced a GPMG position which had pinned them down just below the summit.[4]

> **Metre by metre 5 platoon clawed its way upward and finally silenced a GPMG position**

Back on the southern slopes, 6 Platoon, which had succeeded in establishing a precarious toehold on the summit of 'Fly Half', had by now run into trouble. Corporal Steggles had led his 1 Section up towards the summit to hunt down an Argentine mortar which lay beyond whilst Corporal Wilson and Lance Corporal Murdoch had directed their sections east to winkle out the Argentine sangars just below the crest. In the darkness and confusion 6 Platoon had bypassed a bunker holding at least seven men. Dotted elsewhere on the mountain were snipers with state of the art second-generation passive night sights. As Corporal Murdoch's section worked forward, they veered north, working towards the reverse slopes of 'Fly Half' which marked the western rim of the broad saddle of lower ground between 'Fly Half' and 'Full Back' and known as 'The Bowl'. As they crossed a strip of open ground they came in range of an Argentine sniper further east along the crest towards 'Full Back'. Lance Corporal Murdoch was hit and fell to the ground. Still alive, he lay exposed in the open.

> *'When you go past things there could be hidden trenches but you just do not see them and remember, it's night time as well. There's a threat coming from any area so you're advancing all the time and when you're going past, 'bang' there's blokes who are shooting at you from behind because you haven't seen the defensive position. But we were being opened up on from*

The battle errupts. As B Company advance towards their objective, 'Fly Half', Coporal Brian Milne steps on an anti-personnel mine. The explosion alerts the Argentine soldiers and Longdon explodes in a blizzard of tracer. This image was taken from the left of 4 Platoon's forward left section. Military Picture Library International

> **There's 'incoming' everywhere, loads of stuff going down the range and then 'bang' my pal 'Fester' gets it just above his left eye**

the sides as well. We'd moved forward and were behind a rocky outcrop. Pete Grey stood up and went to throw a '42' grenade and he was shot by a sniper in his right forearm. We thought the grenade had gone off. We punched his arm down into the ground to staunch the bleeding, believing he'd lost half his right forearm and hand, but it was still there and his arm bent at the forearm instead of at the elbow- a horrible thing to watch. We were laying fire down because by this time Trev and the guys - including 'Doc' Murdoch - had been pinned down by a sniper. There's 'incoming' everywhere, loads of stuff going down the range and then 'bang' my pal 'Fester' [Tony Greenwood], gets it just above his left eye, only a yard away from me. That was a terrible thing. 'Fester' was such a lovely guy. Then it was 'Baz' Barratt. 'Baz' had gone back to try and get field dressings for Pete Grey and as he was coming back 'bang' he got it in the back. This was when we just stalled as a platoon. There was no further we could go. The snipers were just picking people off. It was very difficult and we suffered. It was a sniping battle in that respect. So it was like 'go firm'. Every time I went to engage - I knew where these people were - it

Two helmets and rifles break the skyline, marking the spot where Corporal Murdoch and Private Stewart 'Geordie' Laing were shot dead by an Argentine sniper. Military Picture Library International

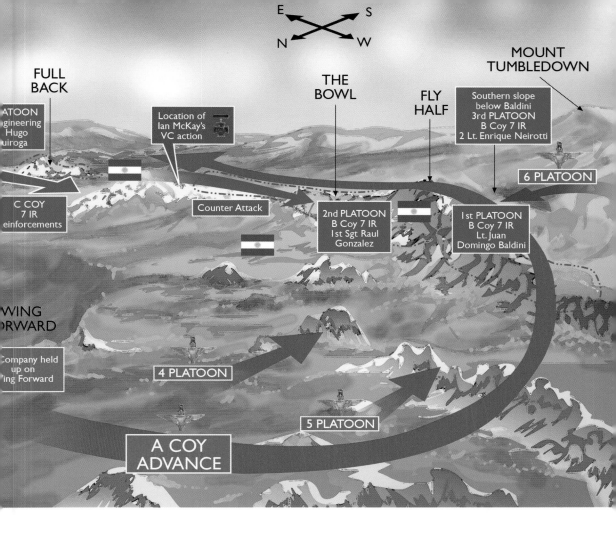

E   S

N   W

FULL
BACK

MOUNT
TUMBLEDOWN

ATOON
gineering
Hugo
uiroga

Location of
Ian McKay's
VC action

THE
BOWL

FLY
HALF

Southern slope
below Baldini
3rd PLATOON
B Coy 7 IR
2 Lt. Enrique Neirotti

6 PLATOON

C COY
7 IR
einforcements

Counter Attack

2nd PLATOON
B Coy 7 IR
1st Sgt Raul
Gonzalez

1st PLATOON
B Coy 7 IR
Lt. Juan
Domingo Baldini

WING
ORWARD

Company held
up on
ing Forward

4 PLATOON

5 PLATOON

A COY
ADVANCE

A British sniper in a ghillie suit. Illustrated by Jon Wilkinson

was 'zzzum'. That deters you from sticking your head around the rocks too often. There was green tracer as well, which was all wrong. Hey! our tracer's not green! Course it's not, its theirs, its coming at you and in between every one of those [tracer rounds] there's another two or three or four, so you keep your head down. So you've got all this noise, you've got men howling and screaming and five or six yards away there's an abandoned Argentine radio set chattering away in Spanish! 'Doc' Murdoch was killed there. Oh man! I really think he was being toyed with by that guy. Shot him in the thigh first of all, then he shot him in the arm; shot him in the side of the head which blinded him. 'Doc' was telling us all this. We could hear him dying. It was terrible - a horrible way to die, a haunting way. A brave man.'

'It was like a football match when you want to join in and help your side.'

6 Platoon B Company, 3 Para, were indeed suffering. To add to 6 Platoon's misery, the weight and accuracy of the Argentine fire and subsequent attempts to locate the sources, had altered its axis and it had strayed north, into the crossfire of a heavy machine gun firing on Lieutenant Cox's 5 Platoon. As medics frantically moved amongst the rocks trying to tend the wounded, others decided they could not leave their comrades out in the open to suffer any longer. Responding to Corporal Murdoch's cries, Private Stewart Laing broke cover and dashed out to rescue Murdoch only to be struck three times in the chest. He died instantly. This level of casualties - 5 dead and eight wounded, almost 50% of Lieutenant Shaw's command - could not be sustained. Shaw asked for and got permission from Major Argue to 'go firm' - to consolidate and hold the ground taken on the northern slopes.

Over on the left flank of B Company's attack, 4 Platoon had managed to edge forward up Longdon's northern face, hitting the right hand sections of Lieutenant Baldini's command. The right hand section of Lieutenant Andrew Bickerdike's platoon had also been forced into some of the treacherous rock gullies, which diverted them into 5 Platoon's sector but on the left their approach had been across 'dead ground' concealed from the Argentines. With some of 4 Platoon now working up behind 5 Platoon the men on the left pushed on, reaching positions forward of the summit and even began to penetrate the Argentine positions held by First Sergeant Gonzales's 2nd Platoon beyond the northern entrance to 'The Bowl'. Here they found themselves co-mingled with the leading edge of 5 Platoon. One remaining 12.7mm heavy machine gun on the eastern lip of 'The Bowl', towards 'Full Back' to the east and holding up the final push for the summit, was silenced when Privates Gray and Gough (5 Platoon), under covering fire from Lance Corporal Carver and Private Juliff, took the bunker at the point of the bayonet. Having cleared the way this far, the mixed force of 4 and 5 Platoons were now sheltering among the rock outcrops around the rim of 'The Bowl' trying to identify the next line of defence before descending to the relatively open saddle of ground leading to their final objective, 'Full Back'. That next line of defence was to prove formidable. Sited in depth, in a classic reverse slope position, were at least two 7.62mm GPMG positions, one heavy Marine Infantry machine gun supported by Marine Infantry riflemen with night sights and a 105mm anti-tank, recoilless rifle.

The battle had been raging now for some two hours. As soon as the paras began to move down from the crest, the accumulation of Argentine firepower, much of it pre-plotted, from sangars around and beyond a second 'Bowl' rocked their advance every time they tried to move. Lieutenant Bickerdike's Platoon HQ came under heavy fire and Bickerdike was hit in the thigh whilst Private Cullen, his radio operator, was caught in the mouth by the same burst. There were at least three other casualties, including Private Neil Grose who had turned eighteen that day. These men badly needed medical aid and fire support but the planned fire support base that should by now have been established by A Company and Support Company on 'Wing Forward' had not materialised. Major Collett's Company and the sustained fire GPMG and Milan sections under Major Dennison's command, had reached 'Wing Forward' but had come under sustained and accurate fire from several snipers in Sergeant Gonzalez's 2nd Platoon area whilst Argentine 155mm and 105mm howitzer rounds fell amongst them. Sheltered behind low banks of earth most of the men had gone to ground and were trying to engage the snipers whenever they had the opportunity. Corporal Vincent Bramley remembers seeing the firefight erupt on the mountain and his feelings of frustration at being unable to influence the outcome, 'It was like a football match when you want to join in and help your side.'[5]

> ...the paras fought through with rifle and bayonet and moved towards the crest of the ridge...

Both A and Support Companies could see what was happening, but pinned down as they were, they were not in a position to intervene effectively. In any event those few who were in a position to engage the Argentines on the mountain were afraid of hitting their own men fighting from right to left across their immediate line of fire. It was clear that the Argentines were not packing up and running to Stanley. They were, in the main, standing and making a fight of it. At some point during the battle on the western slope, Lieutenant Juan Baldini had fired a GPMG on the western slopes until it jammed and he was charged by a group of paras. Drawing a pistol he fired 13 shots in their direction before they reached him. He was later found dead half in, half out of sangar with his pistol in his hand and no boots on his feet.[6]

The advance, it seemed, was stalling at all points. The struggle was being distilled into a bloody battle of attrition. In order to secure victory the men on both sides would have to dig deep and call on hidden depths of determination and the ability to endure to the end. There could be no 'draw' on this mountain. Something out of the ordinary was required if the initiative was to be regained.

Lieutenant Bickerdike's Platoon Sergeant, Ian McKay, now assumed command of the composite force from his own platoon and the left section of 5 Platoon under Corporal Bailey, clinging to their precarious gains beyond the second 'Bowl'. Conferring with Corporal Bailey, Sergeant McKay identified a heavy 50 cal machine gun at the heart of the Argentine defences that was thwarting any attempt to move along the central spine of the ridge. The next cover was thirty-five metres away and

SERGEANT McKAY

Sergeant Ian John McKay was awarded the Victoria Cross for his action on Mount Longdon. His citation reads:

'It was clear that instant action was needed if the advance was not to falter and increasing casualties to ensue. Sergeant McKay decided to convert this reconnaissance into an attack in order to eliminate the enemy positions...He issued orders and taking three men with him, broke cover and charged at the enemy position. The assault was met by a hail of fire. The corporal was seriously wounded, a private killed and another wounded. Despite these losses, Sergeant McKay continued to charge the enemy position alone. On reaching it he despatched the enemy with grenades, thereby relieving the position of beleaguered 4 and 5 Platoons...Sergeant McKay, however, was killed at the moment of victory, his body falling on the bunker. Without doubt, Sergeant McKay's action retrieved a most dangerous situation and was instrumental in ensuring the success of the attack. His was a coolly calculated act, the dangers of which must have been too apparent to him beforehand. With a complete disregard for his own safety, he displayed courage and leadership of the highest order, and was an inspiration to all those around him.'

there were several layers of protective bunkers and two further GPMGs between the paras and the heavy machine gun emplacement. Gathering together Corporal Bailey and three more men - Lance Corporal James, Private Burt and another private - and calling for suppressive fire, McKay's group charged across the open to be met by a hail of fire. Private Burt was killed almost immediately and Lance Corporal James was driven into cover but McKay, Bailey and the other private kept going, grenading and firing into a sangar without stopping until Corporal Bailey, shot in the hip, staggered and fell. The last person to see Sergeant McKay alive was Corporal Bailey who watched from his prone position as he ran on alone towards the Argentine machine gun nest until he disappeared. Bailey was then hit twice more. The machine gun fell silent. After the battle Sergeant Ian McKay's body was found lying amongst the human wreckage of an Argentine bunker. For his actions on Longdon that night Sergeant McKay was awarded a posthumous Victoria Cross, the second such award to the Parachute Regiment in two weeks.[7]

With the hard core of resistance broken, 4 and 5 Platoons could now move once more although the Argentine fire from further positions towards 'Full Back' was still intense. With 'Sunray 21' (Bickerdike) and 'Sunray Minor' (McKay) down, Major Argue sent Sergeant Des Fuller forward to co-ordinate the command of 4 Platoon. Moving up the western slopes of the mountain Sergeant Fuller first established the situation on reaching Lieutenant Bickerdike and then, with the aid of Corporal McLaughlin, decided on a 'simple' plan. They would carry on moving forward. And that is what they did. In a series of audacious, ferocious assaults, they moved down the reverse slope into and beyond the second 'Bowl', sangar by sangar, taking casualties until they too could go no further. Just as 6 Platoon had done earlier Sergeant Fuller, his position now bolstered by the steady and uncompromising presence of CSM Weeks, who began to organise the evacuation of the wounded, 'went firm'. Major Argue had by now moved his HQ in among the rocks on the summit of 'Fly Half' and although the situation was far from clear, Major Argue knew enough to appreciate that his company, as it stood, was not going to get much further along the spine of the mountain. 'Fly Half' was, for the moment, secure, but the battalion was only half way to its final objective. Sometime around midnight Major Carrizo-Salvadores ordered the 45 men of his reserve - the 1st Platoon of the 10th Engineer

Private Jim 'Scouse' Pritchard on the morning after the battle for Mount Longdon summit. In the background his colleagues round up Argentine prisoners shrouded in smoke from their burning sangars. Terry Peck.

Lance Corporal Graham Tolson and comrades take a break after the battle on 14 June, as they prepare for the next phase of the war - the advance on Port Stanley.

Terry Peck.

Private 'Baz' Barrett is evacuated from Mount Longdon on the morning after the battle. Barrett went into action just yards away from Nick Rose and was struck in the back by a bullet just above the sciatic nerve.

Tom Smith, Daily Express

Company under Lieutenant Quiroga - forward from its positions around the command post and 'Full Back'. Moving along the crest in the darkness they did not shirk their duty as they headed towards the fighting but they probably did little more than help to shore up a buckling defence just east of 'Fly Half' and extricate the survivors of isolated bunkers. They did not succeed in knocking the paras from their precarious perch on and around the western summit. This was a critical stage in the battle, the outcome of which now hung in the balance.

By about 2.30 a.m. Lieutenant Colonel Pike had managed to move his HQ up onto 'Fly Half' to join Major Argue. He quickly assessed the situation. Fire from Argentine positions on 'Full Back' had checked the frontal assault of 4 and 5 Platoons and every attempt by 6 Platoon to get around the flanks, whilst A Company - still relatively intact - were still being pinned down on 'Wing Forward' to the north east. C Company under Major Osborne was still on 'Free Kick' and would take too long to get into the battle. A radical solution would be necessary if 3 Para were to secure 'Full Back'. Some of the fire support GPMG and Milan teams were already arriving in B Company's positions. Working the problem Pike ordered A Company and the remaining teams of Support Company, to double back to the western end of Longdon, climb up through the ground already captured by B Company and then launch their attack on 'Full Back' along the same axis, bursting through the leading elements of 4 and 5 Platoons. It was a bold scheme.

As A Company made its way back to the lower western slopes Major Argue called down artillery and Naval Gunfire Support from HMS *Avenger* as he pulled his men back from their forward positions and reorganised his battered company for one last effort to break through. Leading a composite force from 4 and 5 Platoons and fire support teams, Lieutenant Cox moved along the northern slopes in a flank attack under cover of *Avenger*'s 4.5 inch barrage, towards the spot where Sergeant McKay had last been seen charging the Argentine machine gun. Cox managed to get his team some way along the track but as the naval gunfire lifted they ran into the same volume of fire that had previously halted B Company's advance. This time, however, the defenders included forty-six fresh reservists of First Lieutenant Raul Fernando Castaneda's 2nd Platoon of C Company, 7 Infantry Regiment which had recently arrived on Longdon from Wireless Ridge. They had arrived a little before 3 a.m. in response to Major Carrizo-Salvadores' request for reinforcements at 1.30 a.m. Castaneda's men joined with those of First Sergeant Gonzalez in resisting Cox's advance but the paras fought through with rifle and bayonet and moved towards the crest of a slope where they exposed themselves to fire from the bunkers

The British flag flies once again in Port Stanley. Men of 3 Para triumphantly hold their banner for the camera at the end of their campaign.

of Lieutenant Neirotti's 3rd Platoon and those clustered around Carrizo-Salvadores' HQ. B Company strength was now down by 50%. They could get no further. It was time for A Company to take up the sword.

With fire support teams ensconced on the eastern slopes of 'Fly Half' as a combined firebase, Major Collett deployed his men for the assault. Covered by five sustained fire GPMGs, a light machine gun and 3 Milan posts acting as 'bunker busters' and the British artillery, Major Collett - drawing lessons from B Company's experiences - ordered his platoons to conduct a slow and methodical advance from sangar to sangar through 'The Bowl', moving one platoon forward at a time. It was time consuming but it was effective as metre by metre the paras searched out and destroyed the Argentine bunkers on their relentless sweep towards 'Full Back'. But although some Argentine troops abandoned their posts many more clung to their positions and held fast on the eastern summit and around Carrizo-Salvadores' HQ. Fire from Mount Tumbledown to the south added further to the paras' difficulties.

The Argentine commander was obliged to move when a Milan scored a near miss and it was men of the Milan teams who became some of the last para fatalities of the battle. It was an artillery round, or a round from a Czekalski 105mm recoilless rifle operated by Corporal Manuel Medina, one of First Lieutenant Castaneda's men, firing along the length of the ridge towards 'Fly Half', that scored a direct hit on the Milan team operated by Corporal Keith McCarthy and Privates Peter Hedicker and Phillip West. Privates Hedicker and West were killed instantly and Corporal McCarthy died a short time later.

With daybreak just a little over an hour away it looked as though Brigadier Thompson's fears of the battle spilling over into daylight hours were about to be realised but A Company's assault gathered pace and as dawn broke Major Collett's men had breached the Argentine defences around 'Full Back' and were almost onto the summit. Major Carrizo-Salvadores' men had fought the paras all night but now, at a little after 6.30 a.m., he finally disengaged and withdrew towards Port Stanley in the half light and mists of dawn with just 78 of the 287 men who had begun the fight. A Company finally moved on 'Full Back' and combed out the last of the Argentine bunkers whilst 3 Platoon went beyond to secure and guard the long slope down to Wireless Ridge. A Company casualties, during the two hours or more it had taken to reach 'Full Back', amounted to one man - Private Coady - wounded by fragments from his own grenade.

Longdon finally belonged to the paras. The battle might have been over but at a dreadful cost. 3 Para's losses amounted to 18 killed and more than 40 wounded, Argentine losses were thought to be 31 killed, 120 wounded and 50 taken prisoner. But as the evacuation of wounded, consolidation and reorganisation got into full swing the first of the Argentine rounds from the direction of Stanley crashed amongst the rocks searching for their targets. This was just the start of the most sustained artillery barrage suffered by any unit of the British Army since Korea in the summer of 1953.[8] More men were yet to die on Longdon. The suffering was not over.

FALKLANDS
MOUNT LONGDON

THE LEGACY

With the coming of the dawn on the morning of 12th June, the immediate aftermath of the Battle for Mount Longdon became apparent. Lieutenant Colonel Hew Pike later recalled the scene which greeted 3 Para as the dawn broke; a scene which provided perhaps the most haunting memory of that long, cold and bitter fight. 'Groups of young soldiers, grim faced, shocked but determined, moved through the mist with their bayonets fixed to check the enemy dead. The debris of battle was scattered along the length of the mountain, encountered round every turn in the rocks, in every gully. Weapons, clothing, rations, blankets, boots,

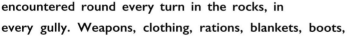

tents, ammunition, sleeping bags, blood soaked medical dressings, web equipment and packs had all been abandoned along with the 105mm recoilless rifles, 120mm mortars, Browning heavy machine guns and the sophisticated night vision binoculars and sights with which Argentinian snipers had given us so much trouble during the long night. The sour and distinctive odour of death lingered in the nostrils as we began to dig temporary graves for some of the enemy dead. But it was a slow job, and eventually the task was abandoned when enemy artillery and mortars started again.' [1]

One of the most painful tasks was the ongoing care of the wounded and the collection and identification of the 3 Para dead. CSM Weeks, who had moved up and down the mountain all night chivvying B Company on and carrying wounded back down the mountain to Colour Sergeant Brian Faulkner's Regimental Aid Post, now faced a task that no one wanted.

'The following morning, when it was light, in between artillery and mortar coming down, we had to go and sort out the bodies and do the documentation. Although it sounds stupid, in battle you still have to account for everything and everybody and you have to fill in the bloody paperwork. I went round to the lads who were left and I asked if any of them would come and help me remove the bodies. I didn't particularly want to do it. I found it terribly hard to ask the guys and they found it terribly hard to say no outright. They tried to make an excuse that they were too busy doing other things rather than say they didn't want to go down to their friends and bring their bodies up. Lewis and Clarkson-Kearsley were the only ones who said they'd come. Sammy Docherty (sic) also came because it needed four to carry a body on a poncho and get them all down to a central place.' [2]

The process of searching the dead for personal effects, removing wedding rings, leaving one dog tag on and filling in forms indicating where wounds had been inflicted was indeed grim but was absolutely essential. Even experienced soldiers

The grim aftermath of battle. British soldiers inspect the body of a fallen Argentine, an unpopular but necessery task which has to be undertaken during any conflict. John Hughes-Wilson.

like CSM Weeks, who admitted to having seen 'loads of dead bodies' during his soldiering, were visibly shaken when tending the bodies of men - men like Sergeant Ian McKay - that they had known well and had come to respect. Colour Sergeant Faulkner's team removed the bodies and all personal effects were handed to the Padre.

As the mist dispersed and Longdon came into view of Argentine artillery observers on Mount Tumbledown, the shelling intensified. With such a level of casualties and with ten hours fighting behind them there would be no further exploitation towards Wireless Ridge. 3 Para would have to sit it out on Longdon and wait for the next move.

The capture of Mount Longdon was of pivotal importance in that it secured and obscured the supply route back towards Teal Inlet, enabling ammunition and supplies to be brought up for phase two of Brigadier Thompson's plan, the assaults on Mount Tumbledown and Wireless Ridge. Just as important, for the wounded of the Longdon battle and those that would follow, its capture meant that they could be casevac'd out without coming under fire. This proved invaluable later as the low cloud on the high ground during the following two days disrupted the evacuation of wounded to Fitzroy. All the Scots Guards casualties evacuated from the Battle of Tumbledown were treated at 3 Commando Brigade Forward Dressing Station at Teal Inlet.

> 'With hindsight I would have used naval gunfire to engage enemy batteries throughout.'

So could anything have been done differently? In his book published to coincide with the twentieth anniversary of the outbreak of the war, Graham Colbeck, a Sergeant in charge of a Milan section on Longdon in 1982, questioned both the lack of artillery preparation in the overall Brigade plan and the use of all three platoons of B Company being used together in 'line abreast' in the battalion plan.[3] Colbeck and other Longdon veterans have pointed to the reliance on surprise rather then firepower as the reason for the battle grinding on for so long at such a heavy price in killed and wounded.[4] The decision to take on a company strength defence with a company (B) - rather than stacking the odds in 3 Para's favour by using more men and the lack of a dedicated 'reserve' platoon for that company once it became engaged by the Argentine's is another source of contention. All three platoons of B Company became stalled almost simultaneously in the face of heavy, well-sited and increasingly accurate firepower, hence there were too few men left with which to 'reinforce success' at any point on the western slopes. There were, as has already been discussed previously, very good reasons why the brigade and battalion plans were developed as they were. Both Lieutenant Colonel Pike and Brigadier Thompson admitted to have been lulled into an overoptimistic assessment of the nature of the Argentine defences and their ability to defend Longdon due to the runaway success of 3 Para's preparatory patrolling. This goes a long way to explaining why there was such a reliance on surprise rather than firepower. However, and it is essential here to embrace the entire canvas on which the strategy of 3 Commando Brigade was painted and extend the picture beyond the outer crust of the phase one Stanley defences. It was deemed essential for

Longdon to be silent so as to mask the northern axis of approach and to conserve vital stocks of ammunition for a war which, for all Brigadier Thompson knew, may well have taken weeks more rather than the two days as it turned out. If there was one thing Brigadier Thompson would have employed differently, if he were to plan phase one all over again, it would be naval gunfire, as opposed to artillery support, for which there was precious little excess ammunition available anyway.

> *'With hindsight I would have used naval gunfire to engage enemy batteries throughout. Also I would have suggested that night harassing tasks by naval gunfire was a waste of ammunition, and kept it for a really concentrated crack at the enemy artillery.'* [5]

The debate will go on. Perhaps if Brigadier Thompson had used his naval gunfire support en masse to engage the Argentine batteries from the four ships available to him, rather than dispersing it between the attacking formations, then there is the possibility that some of the batteries which began to fire defensively on Longdon almost as soon as it became clear to the Argentines that the mountain had been lost, may have been neutralised. It is yet another in the long line of military history's 'what ifs'.

As it was from around 8.00 a.m. on the morning of 12th June the Argentine artillery pounded 3 Para for the next 36 hours and claimed the lives of a further 5 members of the battalion, including Corporal Stewart McLaughlin and Private Richard Absolon (Military Medal), both of whom had assumed prominent roles during the night's fighting. In all, 23 men were killed during the battle for Mount Longdon and the subsequent shelling. 47 men were wounded, some of them with terrible injuries, including the loss of limbs. For those who had emerged unscathed - physically at least - they would watch as their sister battalion, 2 Para, seized Wireless Ridge to the east on the night of 13th/14th June, before charging into Port Stanley hard on 2 Para's heels for the honour of being the first Para battalion to reach the capital after the formal Argentine surrender on 14th June. It was in billets in deserted sheds, houses and in the grandstand of the racecourse to the west end of Stanley that 3 Para's war ended, officially at least.

Corporal Stewart 'Scouse' McLaughlin. A 'soldier's soldier' to his men, his influence during the battle was marked by his fearless tenacity.

*Argentine POWs march towards a ship which will take them home after the
Falklands campaign.*

But men cannot live through a battle like Longdon and not be affected. 14th June
1982 was just the date when the real fighting ended. For many the internal battle,
the mental battle - as they grappled to comprehend what they had seen, heard and
felt - had only just begun, although in the euphoria of staying alive to witness victory
they could not know it.

Just over a decade after the end of the campaign, as men began to record their
personal accounts and experiences of the war, allegations of war crimes and
atrocities committed against the Argentine dead and prisoners of war, and of the
summary execution of 'American' mercenaries surfaced in a book called *Excursion
to Hell* by Vincent Bramley. Bramley had been a corporal in Major Dennison's
Support Company during the battle. The revelations contained in its pages
eventually attracted the attention of politicians and investigative journalists. Such
was the controversy surrounding them that an investigation headed by detective
superintendent Alec Edwards of the Serious and International Crimes section of
New Scotland Yard was initiated in 1992. Even as early as 1982, those responsible
for screening Argentine prisoners prior to repatriation in 1982, had found no
evidence to substantiate the claims that American mercenaries had taken part in the
Longdon battle.[6] After two years of the enquiry during which time, key witnesses
were taken back to Longdon, the Director of Public Prosecutions ruled that the

findings of the investigation were inconclusive and that no charges were to be brought.[7] Nevertheless, for those struggling to come to terms with life after the war, be they still in the regiment or trying to earn a living on 'civvy street', it was a time of deep unease. That night on Longdon would never be forgotten - it was, it is, still with them, every night for some, vividly recalled in the recurring nightmares they were and are experiencing - and their sense of regimental and personal pride and the memory of their dead comrades had somehow been tarnished. Was an investigation necessary? Most certainly. Once the revelations had passed from the realm of British Army folklore and into the public domain with the help of the media, there was never any question that the veracity of the claims would not be tested. Any nation that respects the rule of law, actively promotes justice and upholds human rights cannot ignore such serious allegations. War, however, is quite literally, a bloody and brutal business that extracts its own price from those engaged in it. Personalities are hammered out on the anvil of battle and the supercharged mixture of aggression, ruthlessness, adrenalin and fear cannot simply be switched on and off like a tap. Some crumble, others come through; all are changed and not always for the better. There can be no excuse for the execution of unarmed prisoners of war in cold blood but the battlefield, by its very nature, is a world set apart from the rest of civilised society for the duration of the struggle. The very nature of combat flies in the face of rationality while instinct and the personal 'red mist' that so often descends and drives the soldier on coalesces with the 'fog of war' to cloud the judgment and blur the boundaries. As Graham Colbeck summed up after almost twenty years of considering what happened that night:

> 'Battle is a delicate business between extremes of human behaviour - selfish cowardice and selfless sacrifice, brutality and humanity, callousness and pity - and the virtuous must be made to outweigh the dishonourable, both in the individual and the unit, if either is to survive with any pride.' [8]

Twelve years on from the enquiry and some of the men of Longdon are still battling with their memories. It will stay with them forever. Organisations like Combat Stress, the ex-servicemen's mental welfare association, has provided support and advice for men like Nick Rose who, at the age of twenty, witnessed the death of several close friends on the southern slopes of Longdon.

> 'I do have this PTSD thing but then I think everybody's got it; its just how it manifests itself and how folk deal with it. It's a normal reaction to an abnormal event. But I've suffered with nightmares and I know other people who've gone through the same. It lives with people, especially around Remembrance Day, obviously. But its also a pride thing, I'll always come back to that. The Falklands War was our last colonial war if you like and I fought in it and we won it. I'm proud of that. Extremely so and I'm proud to say I was there. It's sad sometimes but I talk about it with other like-minded people and I get a bit of help. I don't know if I want to go back down yet. I don't think I've got that many ghosts that would warrant me going back down there. I'd like to see it and one day of course, I will. I'd like to take my sons there when they're old enough to understand but it's not about laying ghosts to rest. I think I've done that from here. I like

to think so anyway'

Nick Rose has recently decided to try to raise funds by enlisting the aid of Ken Peers and the Band of the Royal Marines along with several personalities who have offered to record war poetry on CD in aid of the organisation which has helped him to make sense of what happened. He knows he still has some way to go but by getting involved in a project which will help raise public awareness of the organisation's work and much needed funds to help men like him, who gave so much, he hopes that he can at least begin to 'give something back'.

THE EVOLUTION OF A SOLDIER

By Tim Lynch

Tym Lynch served in the Falklands with 159 Army Air Corps. He returned to the Islands for the first time in twenty years in 2002 on the 20th anniversary pilgrimage organised by the South Atlantic Medal Association.

Former US Marine James Jones calls it 'the evolution of a soldier'. It is the moment in combat when you know, with absolute certainty that you are going to die. It is the moment that all the training has been leading to. You go forward to the objective, to help your mates, to do what you are supposed to do but you know that the next step you take will be your last. Those who don't feel that fear aren't heroes, real heroes are those who feel it but go on anyway. For every one of the tired young men on the summit of Mount Longdon, that moment had arrived and they had faced it. Now, as the sun rose over the rocks of East Falkland, they were alive.

The men of 3 Para were exhilarated. This had been the moment they had been waiting for. They had fought their first real battle and won. They had passed what they considered their ultimate test. A US Army study published after WW2 by Colonel S.L.A. Marshall looked into the effectiveness of US infantrymen in the period 1943-45 and found only 15% of trained combat riflemen used their weapons in battle - the rest did not run away, but even under attack they would not kill. 'The thing is simply this,' wrote Marshall 'that out of an average one hundred men along the line of fire during the period of an encounter, only fifteen men on average would take any part with the weapons. This was true whether the action was spread over a day, or two days or three. In the most aggressive infantry companies, under the most intense local pressure, the figure rarely rose above 25% of total strength from the opening to the close of an action'. Training of infantrymen changed as a result of this. Modern combat training was about teaching the recruit to fear letting his mates down more than anything else. The Paras had trained to value aggression and to some, the bayonet fighting on Longdon had been 'a joy'.

So what was the deciding factor in the fight for Longdon? Undoubtedly the long exposure to the elements, coupled with heavy bombardments had taken its toll.

Poor re-supply arrangements had increased the misery for the defenders but, as we have seen, the attackers were also cold, wet, tired and hungry. The major difference between the two forces was about leadership.

Conscripts are capable of fighting extremely well and have done so many times. In the Falklands war, though, two factors came into play. One was that the Argentine military underestimated the speed and nature of the response and had assumed that it would be supplying a garrison force. Consequently, the defenders included a relatively high proportion of logistical and supply troops made up of conscripts who had been poorly prepared for that role which then hampered the supply lines. Secondly, and far more importantly, class distinctions were strictly enforced throughout the military. After the war, for example, Argentine officers and NCOs were bemused by the spectacle of their British counterparts lining up for food behind the ordinary soldiers. Very clear and strict boundaries existed between the conscripts and regular troops and between ranks. Among conscripts, initiative and personal responsibility were neither recognised nor encouraged and this had a significant bearing on their behaviour in combat.

For the Paras aggression is built into training and is highly prized. The problem for them was not that of firing their weapons but of supplying enough ammunition to keep doing so. By contrast, some Argentine veterans report taking shelter and hearing British troops passing literally over the tops of their bunkers. There were reports of conscripts having been disabled by their own officers to prevent them from retreating and the lack of officers and NCOs among Argentine casualties is notable (of 36 Argentines killed on Longdon and Wireless Ridge, one lieutenant and two corporals are listed. The rest were privates. Of the British casualties on Longdon alone, 10 of the 23 killed were NCOs).

Jon Cooksey recounts the assault of 4 and 5 Platoons of B Company towards the northern face of Mt Longdon. The stainless steel memorial cross marking the summit of 'Fly Half' is on the highest point above his head.

The battle won, 3 Para began to relax. In *Excursion to Hell*, Vincent Bramley recalls what happened next. 'We all hit the ground...as the shell landed. No sooner had I started to pick myself up when a high-pitched scream rushed into my ears, a deadly sound. I can still hear it today.' A few metres away, an incoming mortar round had exploded among a group of Paras. Running to help, Bramley 'only saw Denzil, Denzil the character we all loved. I wrenched my eyes to his legs: one was hanging off, ripped to shreds, the bone clearly visible.' Denzil Connick was the only survivor of the group. 'It took nearly a year after this war for Craig's [Jones] face to go before I slept, nearly a year to wipe out Denzil's smock on fire and his scream. Until I die, it will remain a part of me.'

Valuable military lessons were learned from the Longdon battle. Lessons about adequate fire support and about strategy. But the survivors also learned about themselves. As S.A. Stouffer, in a survey of two thousand American troops in the Pacific theatre in 1944, looked at how fear manifested itself. It showed that 84% said they experienced a violent pounding of the heart, others felt sick. About half said they felt faint. A quarter said they had vomited and 21% admitted to having lost control of their bowels. Since this figure is based on voluntary admissions, we could perhaps expect the true figure to be higher. Among themselves, the veterans of 3 Para could privately admit that some things about war had not changed. To outsiders, though, they were Paras. That meant maintaining a reputation. On the way to the South Atlantic, British journalists Patrick Bishop and John Witherow had observed training sessions with some disquiet. They described one in their book *The Winter War*: "What do you do if you find a wounded Argie?" asked a Para corporal, rhetorically, to a platoon weapons talk. "You blow his f—ing head off. What do you do if there's a TV crew watching? You treat him as one of your own". Many of the Toms, as the Para officers called their men with a mixture of affection and contempt, enjoyed their image as emotionless, efficient killers, one step away from being psychopaths. I asked one what he would do if he found a wounded Argie. "Kill him with me bayonet, rip

A rust encrusted 105mm Recoilless Rifle, stands in an abandoned Argentine position in 2002, twenty years after the battle for Mount Longdon. Tim Lynch

his gold teeth out and cut off his fingers to get his rings", he replied. Of course, they did nothing of the sort when the hypothesis became real. But they would like you to think they would.'

It came as no surprise, then, to the rest of the Task Force when rumours of the murder of prisoners on Longdon began to circulate. The stories, which even reached the Falkland Islands newspaper *Penguin News*, were roundly ignored by the many journalists on the Islands, until the same allegations became part of a war crimes investigation over ten years later.

Trained to see themselves as emotionless killers, praised for their aggression and having come to see themselves as dead men, the teenagers of Longdon were ready to go home. Trying to make sense of his own experiences in the Pacific campaigns of WW2, Jones described this evolution as a special kind of moment. 'It is absolutely true' he wrote 'that when you think, when you know, you are going off to die somewhere soon, every day has a special, bright, delicious, poignant taste to it that normal days in normal times do not have. Some men like to live that way all the time. Some are actually sorry to come home and see it end. Even those of us who hated it found it exciting sometimes. That is what civilian people never understand about their returning soldiers. They cannot understand how we could hate it, and still like it; and they do not realise they have a lot of dead men around them, dead men who are walking around and breathing. Some men find it hard to come back from their evolution of a soldier. Some never come back at all, not completely.' Facing the survivors of 3 Para was a problem that had affected generations of soldiers before them. How do you live a life you've already given up on?

Returning Paras, cooped up on board the MV *Norland*, celebrated Airborne Forces Day, 1982 with a drink fuelled riot that continued into the early hours. Sent on leave with the advice to 'get drunk and forget it', they went home to their families. 'Instead of talking about it' remembered Jones of the men who came home in 1945, 'most men didn't talk about it. It was not that they didn't want to talk about it; it was that when they did, nobody understood. It was such a different way of living, and of looking at life even, that there was no common ground for communication in it.' Brought up to believe that returning soldiers 'didn't want to talk about it', the teenage veterans kept quiet. 'I was 19 when I got home' says one, 'and I felt older than my dad. He'd been in the army for years but never heard a shot fired. What could I talk to him about?'. Others, 17 or 18 years old when they got back found that tabloid propaganda had built up public sympathy that lay with the 'young kids' they had faced. Much was made in the British press at the time of the war about the age of the Argentinean troops but in fact, most were drawn from the 'Class of '62' - men born in 1962 and coming to the end of their period of national service. The Task Force, too, was a young unit, the youngest sailor aboard HMS *Invincible* was just 16. Among 3 Para's losses during the attack on Mount Longdon, were three seventeen year-old privates who had only recently joined the battalion. After the war, British veterans found a great deal of sympathy back home for the 'poor Argentine kids' they had faced in battle but a great many returned still too young to buy a legal drink in a pub to celebrate their survival or to vote for the government which had sent them to fight.

The return to ordinary soldiering was not easy and many veterans found themselves disillusioned when 'shiny arses' were promoted over those who had fought well. One by one, they began to leave the army to return to civilian life.

In 1974, the American psychologist Robert Lifton wrote about the case of 'Skip' Johnson, a Vietnam veteran and Medal of Honor winner. Johnson, awarded the medal for hunting down and killing a Vietnamese anti-tank team, found himself unable to cope with having been honoured for, as he saw it, having lost control and killing in a rage. He was killed during an armed robbery in New York. His mother told the press 'sometimes I wonder if he just got tired of living and wanted someone else to pull the trigger'. Just as in the aftermath of Vietnam, from the mid 1980's, stories begin to emerge in the media of Falklands veterans. Tales of alcoholism, drug use, involvement in crime and suicide surfaced on a regular basis and, five years after the war, a study by a Parachute regiment medical officer found that 50% of those veterans still serving were experiencing some or all of the symptoms of Post Traumatic Stress Disorder. If the figure among this group was so high, what was happening to those who had left the army?

The British Ministry of Defence prided itself that the Falklands War had produced very few psychiatric casualties. The short duration of the campaign and high level of training meant that neither army suffered significant losses through 'shell shock'. This was true, only 16 psychiatric casualties were recorded, 2% of the total. Unfortunately, whether by ignorance or design, military psychiatrists, particularly those attached to the Army, failed to grasp the concept of psychological consequences surfacing after combat and continued to concern themselves only with breakdown in combat itself, a very different matter.

Veterans and health care professionals have criticised the MOD for this. Roderick Orner, a psychologist working with Falklands veterans, has described the MOD's failure to recognise the effects of Post Traumatic Stress as 'inexcusable' and criticises its 'shameful record' of providing support to ex-servicemen. The existence of the disorder had been recognised for many years following work among survivors of natural disasters, accidents and particularly among veterans of the Vietnam war and was formally identified by the American Psychiatric Association in 1980, two years before the Task Force set sail. With the honourable exception of Navy Psychiatrist Commander Morgan O'Connell, no attempt was made to address the problem or even to consider it. Interviewed a few months after the war, O'Connell told The Guardian that whilst there had been only 16 psychiatric casualties during the war, in the aftermath he had already treated over a hundred. Having left the Navy in frustration over the way it had treated its veterans, Dr. O'Connell argues that the 'government's uncaring attitude and its policy of ignoring the fact that PTSD is affecting their soldiers, is inflicting more damage on their own men than any foreign power or terrorist organisation could hope to achieve'. It was not until 1986 that the army acknowledged the existence of PTSD and even then argued that civilian resources should be used to treat veterans who had left the forces. Unfortunately, as Dr. O'Connell puts it; 'The NHS has no adequate system for treating [these] men because they usually need to be with their peer group and relate to people who understand the realities of war and service life'.

Studies of Post Traumatic Stress in combat veterans across the world showed that they were 50% more likely to commit suicide and 48% more likely to die in car accidents than those who had not served. They were over represented in the prison system and the British homeless charity SHELTER claimed that 25% of the long-term homeless were ex-servicemen. Twenty years after Longdon, it was estimated that more veterans had died by their own hand than were killed in action. Yet, almost uniquely, Britain refused to accept that its war veterans deserved any special recognition. In answer to this, the veterans began to turn to each other for the help they needed to come to terms with their experiences. Fifteen years after the end of the war, the South Atlantic Medal Association (SAMA) was launched. It was the brainchild of 3 Para veteran Denzil Connick, the man who lost a leg in the mortar attack Bramley witnessed on Longdon on 12th June 1982.

The granite memorial on Mount Longdon blooms with metal poppies in rememberance of the Paras killed during the battle. Tim Lynch

With the help of the people of the Falkland Islands, SAMA set out to mark the 20th anniversary of the end of the war with a pilgrimage by veterans. Refused help by the Ministry of Defence, an aircraft was chartered privately to take 200 survivors back to the battlefields to try to find some answers and some peace. For all the veterans, this was a personal journey to revisit their part of the war and, hopefully, to lay ghosts that had haunted them for years. It was an opportunity to walk again over ground last covered under fire. For some, decisions they had made at the time had earned them criticism and this was a chance to look again at what happened and why. For the common soldier, war is reduced to what happens in his immediate vicinity and he relies on historians to tell him what he did later. For the SAMA veterans, marines mixed with paras and guardsmen to talk about their war and to help fill in the details. It was the debriefing they had never been given. Perhaps most importantly, it was a chance to find the answer to the question that had been uppermost in all our minds since 1982 - was it worth it?

On 11th November 2002, a group gathered on top of Mount Longdon for an act of remembrance. Among them, and now an honorary paratrooper, was former Islands policeman Terry Peck, who had guided them across the islands to this bleak hilltop overlooking Port Stanley. Quietly they made their way up the hillside, following the route they had taken all those years ago. Almost unerringly finding the rocks they had sheltered behind in a landscape burned into their memories, gently placing wreathes on spots where friends had died.

Denzil Connick had never been baptised. He decided it was the right time and that this was the right place. On the way to the Islands in 1982, he had befriended a Marine, David Devenney. Today, Devenney is an ordained minister and proudly conducted a service among the rocks atop Longdon near the spot where Denzil had taken his last real steps. For a moment, the wind eased and silence fell. For the first time in twenty years, the survivors of 3 Para had found peace.

SAMA pilgrimage 2002. Ex-Marine Reverend David Devenney baptizes Denzil Connick on the summit of Mount Longdon. Tim Lynch

3 Para veterans pose for the camera in front of the Mount Longdon memorial cross. Tim Lynch

HEALING THE SOUL
THE ARGENTINE PERSPECTIVE
By Michael Savage

Michael Savage belonged to C Company of the Argentine 7th Infantry Regiment positioned on a feature just north east of Longdon called 'Rough Diamond.' His mortar supported Lieutenant Castañeda's unit during its counter attack along Longdon's crest and the subsequent hand-to-hand fighting. After the Paras had cleared 'Full Back' by the morning of the 12th, he and his comrades were trapped in their positions by the British artillery until dusk that evening. The rest of his company had retreated earlier that day. Eventually he managed to escape towards Stanley. Eighteen years later he returned to the Falklands in the company of James Peck, son of Terry, the Islander who had escaped from Stanley and had joined up with 3 Para at Teal Inlet.

Our trip to the Falklands/Malvinas was planned as a way of drawing the curtain on a sad story. I had to go back to the islands to lay the ghosts to rest; I had to return to the scene but I had to see it in normal times, without the horror.

We had the help of a great friend, James Peck, his wife, Carol and his son Joshua. After many failed attempts to buy air fares, James offered to make our reservations and pay for them in the islands and all this was done ten days before our departure. They also offered to put us up in their home, so little by little we completed the jigsaw. It was a long trip to the military base in Mount Pleasant, with stops in Santiago de Chile, Puerto Montt and Punta Arenas.

It was very important but exhausting to take the family: I travelled with my wife Andrea and my two children, Patricio and Maggie. The weather wasn't on our side, as if to remind us at every moment how hard it was to put up with the atrocious, wet conditions and the hunger of those days of war in 1982. It now seems hard to believe that we survived at all.

Approaching the summit of Mount Longdon from the west. Twenty years on Mike Savage and Terry Peck walk towards the craggy feature on the summit to lay a wreath to the fallen of both sides. Terry Peck

View from the summit in 2002 looking east. Port Stanley is in the distance with Mount Tumbledown to the right. The rock features to the left and centre were used as sniper positions. From these positions snipers were able to pick off the advancing men of 3 Para. Terry Peck

ARGENTINE SNIPER
POSITIONS

FULL
FACK

PORT
STANLEY

MOUNT
TUMBLEDOWN

THE AREA WHERE CORPORAL 'DOC' MURDOCH
AND PRIVATE STEWART LAING WERE KILLED. SEE PAGE 66.

View overlooking the 'Bowl' and the sniper positions. In the middle foreground was the Argentine Command Post and heavy mortar positions. Terry Peck

ARGENTINE CP AND
MORTAR POSITIONS

Michael Savage inspects the corroded remains of his cooker. Michael Savage

We stayed with James Peck, an islander and an artist who opened his home and his heart to us. And although the lashing rain continued and it was very windy, the first day there James and I climbed from Moody Brook to our position. The first thing we spotted from a distance was something brown and square, which turned out to be our old cooker.

And right beside it, in the same spot we had left it 18 years ago, as if waiting for me, was a stainless steel cauldron, with two shrapnel holes in it. I used to cook. I think we used to take it in turns, doing weekly shifts that's when we were able to get more food. But it was a terrible thing to go about serving others in the cold, so my mate Roberto Maldonado and I would fill three canteens with 'maté cocido' to use as hot water bottles and we'd have something warm to drink each morning.

At night we'd leave the cauldron just outside the tent. Field mice would often get into it and they'd freeze to death trying to get out. For meals we had 'maté cocido' in the morning, no sugar or bread; a watery soup at midday and at night a thin broth and nothing else. There was never any bread or fruit. We'd get water with our canteens from nearby ponds. We had no option but to pilfer our own provisions. The booty was hidden in empty munition cases that's how we'd fool the officers.

There were also groups of 'sheep hunters', so you could say that there was a primitive form of bartering going on. Even so, I lost 17 kilos. I came home weighing only 55 kilos and to this day I have been unable to forgive the Argentine officers who were in charge of us. It is still possible to make out a depression in the ground where my tent once was. The 'tent' consisted of two canvas cloths which you had to put together to make an improvised shelter. It is impossible to imagine what it was like to be in this rickety structure in a windstorm. Several times in the night it would blow

Remnants of the Argentine Mortar Platoon's stainless steel cauldron which Michael used to convey food to his colleagues. Terry Peck

The weathered remains of Michael's shelter still standing twenty years on. Terry Peck

91

Michael is able to find other relics of the occupation, such as this canteen, next to the rubble of a stone wall, built for protection against weather and British fire. Michael Savage

away, leaving us crying and praying in the rain out of sheer desperation.

Alan Craig, my Argentine trenchmate, remembers that 'once wet, there was no way you could dry your clothes other than to keep them on and dry them with the heat of your body'.

The slabs that held the tent are now covered with peat. The shovel, canteens and canvas are still intact. At first only the important things stood out, but then it was possible to find all sorts of things, partially buried in the peat. I found a tube of toothpaste, a boot brush, a rucksack and razor blades and shrapnel all over the place. The bomb craters are everywhere and are really impressive. Besides, the grass doesn't grow in them, they're black and I wonder how long they will be there to remind those of us who survived how close we had been to death.

Around three metres away was the position of Alan Craig, Adrián Gómez Scher and Sergeant Alcaide. With the passage of time the stone wall that used to be quite big is now only 80 cms high. Here we found a melted ballpoint pen and some shaving cream.

I didn't want to dig about too much, because I felt respect for the place and I wanted to leave it as it was for the day my friends can visit it. I also found the remainings of a twisted kettle and a plate with the insignia 'EA' Argentine Army. The base of a machine-gun was surrounded by shell holes. Anyone who had been there at the time wouldn't have survived.

We also found two 105mm anti-tank guns. It was amazing one of them was carried by me and six other 'colimbas' (conscripts) by hand uphill from Moody Brook, four kilometres away. It took us four days to do it. Now they lie there like dinosaur skeletons; in fact, this place is like an open air museum and it's hard to believe that so much is still intact.

Left to right: Terry Peck, Michael Savage and James Peck sitting in the 'Bowl' discussing the events of 11/12 June 1982. Michael had been a member of the mortar platoon that had fired on 3 Para from the feature known as 'Rough Diamond'. Terry Peck

Michael Savage's children play amongst the trenches which once protected their father. Many Argentines were killed and wounded in this area. Mount Longdon is in the background. Terry Peck

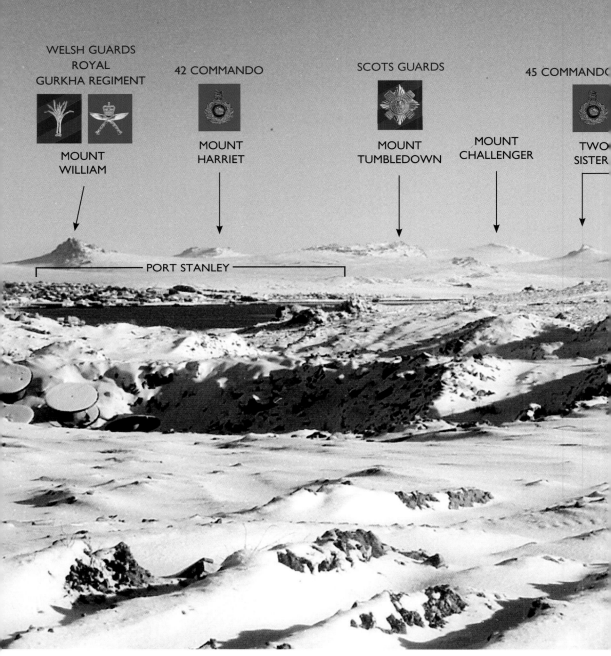

WELSH GUARDS
ROYAL
GURKHA REGIMENT

MOUNT
WILLIAM

42 COMMANDO

MOUNT
HARRIET

SCOTS GUARDS

MOUNT
TUMBLEDOWN

MOUNT
CHALLENGER

45 COMMANDO

TWO
SISTER

PORT STANLEY

The snow capped mountain range barring the way to Port Stanley. Photograph taken looking west from a position across the bay from Port Stanley. Terry Peck

42 COMMANDO
22 SAS - D SQUADRON

MOUNT KENT

3RD BATTALION
PARACHUTE REGIMENT

MOUNT LONGDON

A few days later, James invited his father around. That's how we discovered that Terry is an institution in Stanley. During the Argentine invasion he fled to the hills on his motorbike. For five weeks he lived alone in the open, hiding and eating dried fruit and nuts. Later he joined the 3 Parachute Regiment and guided them to Mount Longdon, where they fought the VII Regiment of LaPlata, which was my regiment. This is where it became really interesting.

We went up the mountain together. We had something in common, that only veterans would understand. We spoke sincerely about what happened on that horrible night of the 11th June, 1982. We filled in the gaps in our stories, exchanging facts and anecdotes.

Terry told me that three days before the battle at Mount Longdon the British were already very close when they saw a group of six men heading for an estancia beyond the Murrell river. An officer suggested kiling them, but the regiment commander stopped them, because this would have alerted the Argentines and they would have lost the surprise element for the attack which was to be carried out the following day. I was among those six men, acting as interpreter.

On the night of the 11th June, B company of the VII Regiment La Plata was awakened when a British soldier stepped on a mine, which gave them some time to prepare. They were on the summit of Mount Longdon; that battle was the fiercest and bloodiest, because it involved 150 men against 150 men.

Just thinking about the battle chills my blood. The English came up a very steep slope towards the Argentine positions; the British mistake was costly and they suffered many losses, so much so that today the battle is analysed and studied in military tactics courses.

From my position I could hear shouting in English and Spanish, tracer bullets,

Port Stanley today. Mount Longdon and Two Sisters in the background.
Tim Lynch

Falklands Summer, Terry and James Peck stand beside the 3 Para memorial. Terry Peck

Terry Peck lays a wreath on the anniversary of the battle each year to remember the Paras who fell in 1982. Terry Peck

everything. In the confusion, C Company of the VII Regiment La Plata, where I was, fired two flares, lighting up the hills. Sub Lieutenant Castañeda organised support for Company B which was under heavy attack.

Castañeda's support was considered by the British to have been one of the most heroic events in the ground fighting on the Malvinas, prompting Brigadier Julian Thompson to say: "I was on the point of withdrawing my paras from Longdon. We couldn't believe that these teenagers disguised as soldiers were causing us to suffer so many losses."

Alan Craig remembers that "that night B company wasn't using radars because they were trying to save batteries."

As for me, I was there when they organised the group, but as I belonged to a mortar support group I wasn't picked. I saw 46 men leave and head straight for Longdon, of whom only 21 returned. They headed out in the dead of night straight into a bloody battle. The heroism of these kids was incredible; those of who remained behind were praying and I couldn't stop trembling.

The next morning as two of the 21 survivors were giving us their account of what had happened, a mortar shell fell two metres from our trench, killing one of them instantly and wounding the other while Roberto, my mate, took a shrapnel wound in the intestines.

"When the artillery started pounding on us, we jumped into this hole, dug into the peat bank. It was constructed by a conscript that was an engineer. It was 2 metres down, and 2 metres into the bank. During the time we were waiting for the attack, it was a very hard job keeping it dry but the reward was great!

This hole saved my life. In the middle of the night the *colimbas* came to ask me how

A gaunt but happy Michael Savage returns from the Falklands to the loving embrace of his mother. His lack of nourishment is clearly evident.

Michael Savage

An emotional return. Now promoted to Major General, Hew Pike OBE, returns to Mount Longdon for the first time in ten years to salute the men of his battalion who fell on Mount Longdon. December 1992. Terry Peck

A plaque in the grounds of Government House, Port Stanley, to mark the 150th anniversary of its establishment. It was important that this was recaptured after the Argentine occupation, as it was a symbol of British sovereignty on the Falkland Islands. Tim Lynch

to say "me rindo" (I surrender) in English and they left for their dugouts repeating the words "I surrendo, I surrendo."

Some of them tried to make white flags but by then we didn't have anything left that was that colour because all our clothes were filthy, black with soot from cooking with helicopter fuel. Getting to know another war veteran, and especially Terry, who was on the other side, was very special. We had both been through the same experience in the war. As we climbed Longdon in a four-wheel-drive vehicle, Terry listened in almost complete silence as I told him how we had spent 60 days in those holes.

At first the British had wanted Terry to guide the regiment to Stanley, but as he is very able with guns, they relented and gave him one and he fought at Longdon on 11th June.

It was very interesting to hear the British side of things. They are very conscious of the battle at Longdon because 23 Britons died there. On the summit there is a cross and a plaque with names. I don't know exactly how many Argentines died there, but we do know it was one of the bloodiest battles.

There are wreathes of poppies to honour the dead, one of them from Prince Charles, who was taken there by Terry. It is so windy on the summit that one can't stay there very long. We moved lower down and had a meal and some brandy from Terry's flask, with its 3 Para insignia engraved on it. And we began to reveal what we didn't know about each other.

The original memorial cross erected on the spot where it was first thought Sergeant Ian McKay had been killed charging an Argentine machine-gun position. It was replaced in July 2012 by the then serving sergeants of B Company, 3 Para during their tour of duty as part of Resident Infantry Company.

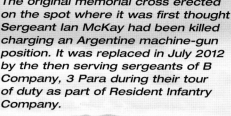

Major General Hew Pike OBE visits Blue Beach cemetery, 1992.

Terry Peck

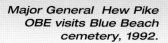

Blue Beach cemetery. Major General Pike pays his respects at the grave of fellow battalion commander of 2 Para, Lieutenant Colonel 'H' Jones. Terry Peck

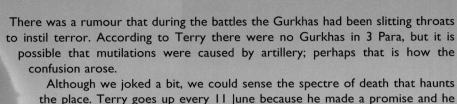

There was a rumour that during the battles the Gurkhas had been slitting throats to instil terror. According to Terry there were no Gurkhas in 3 Para, but it is possible that mutilations were caused by artillery; perhaps that is how the confusion arose.

Although we joked a bit, we could sense the spectre of death that haunts the place. Terry goes up every 11 June because he made a promise and he keeps it, regardless of the weather. Life has given us the opportunity to meet and be friends and we won't waste it. When Terry came to say goodbye, we embraced as friends.

How absurd all war is. It is incredible that, in the times we live in, anyone should think of forcing change on other people's lives. And it's unbelievable that young conscripts should have had to bear the brunt of this epic jaunt, whose prime motivation was nationalist sentiment. It was like plucking people off the street and forcing them to fight a professional army. We have all thanked God that it wasn't our time.

This trip has healed my soul. Spending those 15 days with the Pecks, to be a part of their life, was fundamental. The ghosts of war have gone, only to be replaced by a great friendship. I can't find the words to thank those who opened their homes and their hearts to us.

3 PARA MOUNT LONGDON
11th/12th June 1982
ROLL OF HONOUR

Private R. J. ABSOLON, MM	Private P. J. HEDICKER	Corporal K. J. McCARTHY
Private G. BULL	Lance Corporal P. D. HIGGS	Sergeant I. J. McKAY, VC
Private J. S. BURT	Corporal S. HOPE	Corporal S. P. F. McLAUGHLIN
Private J. D. CROW	Private T. R. JENKINS	Lance Corporal J. H. MURDOCH
Private M. S. DODSWORTH	Private C. E. JONES	Lance Corporal D. E. SCOTT
Private A. D. GREENWOOD	Private S. I. LAING	Private I. P. SCRIVENS
Private N. GROSE	Lance Corporal C. K. LOVETT	Private P. A. WEST

ATTACHED

Craftsman
A. SHAW
Royal Electrical & Mechanical Engineers

Corporal
S WILSON
9 Parachute Squadron Royal Engineers

GALLANTRY AWARDS

Sergeant I. J. McKay, B Coy: V.C. posthumous

Lieutenant Colonel H. W. R. Pike, MBE: D.S.O.

Major M. H. Argue, B Coy: M.C.

Major D. A. Collett, A Coy: M.C.

Colour Sergeant B. Faulkner, Regimental Aid Post: D.C.M.

Sergeant J. S. Pettinger, D Patrol Coy: D.C.M.

Private R. J. de M. Absolon, D (Patrol) Coy: M.M. posthumous

Corporal I. P. Bailey, B Coy: M.M.

Sergeant D. Fuller, B Coy: M.M.

ATTACHED

Captain W. A. McCracken, 29 Commando Regiment Royal Artillery: M.C.

July 2012 and the current B Company, 3 Para visit Mount Longdon to learn of their history. Here the author discusses the fight up the western slopes. Graham Heaton, a corporal who lost his leg in the battle in 1982, can be seen at the summit cross.

Graham Heaton recounts his experiences during the battle to the men of B Company, 3 Para in July 2012 at the summit of Mount Longdon – 'Fly Half'. The Murrell River is in the distance.

Sergeants of B Company, 3 Para, photographed with the new memorial cross in memory of Sergeant Ian McKay VC, which they erected to replace the damaged original in July 2012. The steel memorial cross on 'Fly Half' is clearly visible above.

A fin from an Argentine Cobra anti-tank missile found on Mount Longdon in 2008. Argentine maps show one Cobra deployed before the battle.

An almost full tube of Argentine toothpaste found on Mount Longdon in 2007.

NOTES

INTRODUCTION

1. Duncan Anderson, 'Let's Remember Arnhem' 2 Para and the Battle of Darwin-Goose Green, *Battlefields Review*, 19, 2002, pp. 51.

THE LANDING

1. Graham Colbeck, *With 3 Para to the Falklands* (London: Greenhill Books, 2002) p. 85. See also Julian Thompson, *No Picnic* (London: Cassell, 2001) p. 49.
2. Martin Middlebrook, *The Falklands War 1982* (London: Penguin, 2001) pp. 214-215
3. Colbeck op.cit. p. 95

THE TAB

1. Middlebrook, op.cit. p. 274-277. See also Vincent Bramley, *Excursion to Hell* (London: BCA, 1991) pp.45-46 and Christian Jennings and Adrian Weale, *Green Eyed Boys* (London: Harper Collins, 1996) p.99.
2. Vincent Bramley, op.cit, pp. 45-56. Jennings and Weale, op.cit, pp. 99-102.
3. Duncan Anderson, *The Falklands War 1982* (Oxford: Osprey, 2002) p. 56.

THE PREPARATIONS

1. Jennings and Weale, op.cit. p.p. 110-114
2. Julian Thompson. op.cit, p. 112.
3. Major General Julian Thompson, C.B., O.B.E. E-mail response to editor's query. January 2004. See also Nicholas van der Bijl, *Nine Battles to Stanley* (Barnsley: Leo Cooper, 1999) pp. 164-165.
4. Major General Julian Thompson, C.B., O.B.E. E-mail response to editor's query. January 2004.
5. Vincent Bramley op.cit. p.77.

THE PLAN

1. Colonel Hew Pike D.S.O. M.B.E., *With Fixed Bayonets*, *Elite Magazine*, vol. 2, 20, 1985. pp. 381
2. Graham Colbeck op.cit. pp. 179-180. See also Jennings and Weale, op.cit. pp. 122-123 and Julian Thompson op.cit. p.112.

THE BATTLE

1. Jennings and Weale, op.cit. pp. 126-127. See also David Aldea, *Mount Longdon The Argentinian Story* (www.britains-smallwars.com/Falklands/David/Longdon) Nicholas van der Bijl, op.cit. pp. 171-172, and Max Arthur, *Above All Courage* (London: Sphere) 1987, p.300
2. Vincent Bramley, *Two Sides of Hell* (London: Bloomsbury, 1994) p.137.

3. Ibid. p. 140.

4. Colonel Hew Pike, op.cit. p.384.

5. Vincent Bramley, (1991) op.cit. p. 90.

6. There is some debate regarding the circumstances surrounding Baldini's death. Some accounts maintain that he was asleep when 3 Para's attack went in, whilst others suggest that his boots were removed by one of the paras to replace the universally loathed British regulation issue DMS boots. Criticised by some of his subordinates after the war, Baldini was posthumously recommended for the Heroic Valour Cross, Argentina's highest military decoration. He was in fact awarded the Gallantry in Combat Medal, and his regiment's parade square was named after him. See Jennings and Weale, op.cit.. p.129, van der Bijl, op.cit. p.173 and David Aldea, op.cit.

7. Sergeant Ian McKay's VC was the first to be awarded to a man in 3 Para and was the last VC of the twentieth century. Since then the VC has been awarded to a further four British servicemen for actions in Iraq and Afghanistan, one of them being Corporal Bryan Budd, also of 3 Para, for actions in engaging Taliban fighters in Helmand Province on 20 August 2006. For an extended account of Ian McKay's pre-Falklands service with the Paras see Jon Cooksey, *Falklands Hero - Ian McKay - The Last VC of the 20th Century* (Barnsley: Pen & Sword 2012).

8. Duncan Anderson, op.cit. pp. 65-66.

THE LEGACY

1. Colonel Hew Pike op.cit. p. 391.

2. Max Arthur, op.cit. p. 306.

3. Graham Colbeck op.cit. pp. 179 -182.

4. See also Jennings and Weale, op.cit. pp. 187-188.

5. Major General Julian Thompson, E mail to editor op.cit.

6. Nicholas van der Bijl, op.cit. p. 173.

7. Jennings and Weale op.cit. pp. 177-191.

8. Graham Colbeck op.cit. p.185.

FURTHER READING

Graham Colbeck, *With 3 Para to the Falklands* (London: Greenhill Books, 2002)

Jon Cooksey, *Falklands Hero - Ian McKay - The Last VC of the 20th Century* (Barnsley: Pen & Sword 2012)

Martin Middlebrook, *The Falklands War 1982* (London: Penguin, 2001)

Martin Middlebrook, *The Argentine Fight for the Falklands:* (Barnsley: Pen & Sword Military Classics, 2003)

Julian Thompson, *No Picnic* (London: Cassell, 2001)

Vincent Bramley, *Excursion to Hell* (London: BCA, 1991)

Christian Jennings and Adrian Weale, *Green Eyed Boys* (London: Harper Collins, 1996)

Duncan Anderson, *The Falklands War 1982* (Oxford: Osprey, 2002)

Nicholas van der Bijl, *Nine Battles to Stanley* (Barnsley: Leo Cooper, 1999)

Nicholas van der Bijl, *Argentine Forces in the Falklands* (London: Osprey, 1992)

Max Arthur, *Above All Courage* (London: Sphere 1987)

Vincent Bramley, *Two Sides of Hell* (London: Bloomsbury, 1994)

Mark Adkin, *The Last Eleven* (London: Leo Cooper 1991)

William Fowler, *Battle for the Falklands (I) Land Forces* (London: Osprey, 1982)

WEBSITES:

www.britains-smallwars.com
www.sama82.org.uk
www.naval-history.net/F54longdon.htm

INDEX

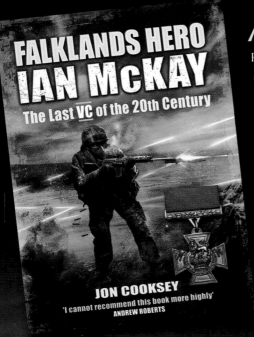